Azure Active Directory for Secure Application Development

Use modern authentication techniques to secure applications in Azure

Sjoukje Zaal

BIRMINGHAM—MUMBAI

Azure Active Directory for Secure Application Development

Copyright © 2022 Packt Publishing

All rights reserved. No part of this book may be reproduced, stored in a retrieval system, or transmitted in any form or by any means, without the prior written permission of the publisher, except in the case of brief quotations embedded in critical articles or reviews.

Every effort has been made in the preparation of this book to ensure the accuracy of the information presented. However, the information contained in this book is sold without warranty, either express or implied. Neither the author, nor Packt Publishing or its dealers and distributors, will be held liable for any damages caused or alleged to have been caused directly or indirectly by this book.

Packt Publishing has endeavored to provide trademark information about all of the companies and products mentioned in this book by the appropriate use of capitals. However, Packt Publishing cannot guarantee the accuracy of this information.

Publishing Product Manager: Rahul Nair

Senior Editor: Shazeen Iqbal

Content Development Editor: Sayali Pingale

Technical Editor: Rajat Sharma

Copy Editor: Safis Editing

Project Manager: Vaidehi Sawant

Proofreader: Safis Editing

Indexer: Rekha Nair

Production Designer: Shankar Kalbhor

Marketing Coordinator: Nimisha Dua

Senior Marketing Coordinator: Sanjana Gupta

First published: May 2022

Production reference: 1110522

Published by Packt Publishing Ltd.
Livery Place
35 Livery Street
Birmingham
B3 2PB, UK.

978-1-83864-650-9

www.packt.com

Contributors

About the author

Sjoukje Zaal is head of the Microsoft Cloud Center of Excellence, a Microsoft Regional Director, and a Microsoft Azure MVP with over 20 years of experience in architecture, development, consultancy, and design-related roles. She currently works at Capgemini, a global leader in consultancy, technology services, and digital transformation. She loves to share her knowledge and is active in the Microsoft community as a cofounder of the user groups Tech Daily Chronicle and Global XR Community. She is also a board member of Azure Thursdays and the Global AI Community. Sjoukje is an international speaker and is involved in organizing many events. She has written several books and writes blogs.

About the reviewers

Swaprakash Sarkar is a technical architect and seasoned professional associated with a multinational technology company. He holds a B.Tech degree in electronics and communication engineering and other professional certifications in Microsoft technology, security, and the cloud. Swaprakash has demonstrated achievements in areas relating to Active Directory, Azure AD, information security, system architecture and design, and project management in his 11-year career in IT. Swaprakash has a passion for learning new technologies that he continues to pursue daily.

Above all the previously stated, he is a father, a husband, a son, a brother, and a friend.

Table of Contents

3

Application Types and User Consent

Part 2: Authentication and Protocols

4

The Basics and Evolution of Authentication

5

Securing Applications with OAuth 2.0, OpenID Connect, and MSAL

6

Building Secure Services Using the Microsoft Graph API

Part 3: Azure AD B2C

7

Introducing Azure Active Directory B2C

8
Advanced Features of Azure AD B2C

9
Azure AD B2C Custom Policies

Index

Other Books You May Enjoy

Preface

Every organization needs protection against cyberattacks and security threats. Cybercrime and malware are constant threats to anyone with an internet presence. Security is one of the most important topics in IT projects nowadays and every developer, architect, and IT professional needs to have some knowledge of it. It is also one of the key elements that spans across every layer in your IT landscape. It needs to be embedded in your infrastructure, data, and applications, among others. That is also the case for cloud environments, such as Microsoft Azure.

This results in Azure Active Directory being the core service inside Azure that ties everything together from an identity and security perspective. The Microsoft identity platform is an authentication service and a layer on top of Azure Active Directory, which provides developers with an authentication service, open source libraries, and application management tools.

Azure Active Directory for Secure Application Development is an in-depth exploration of how Azure Active Directory and the Microsoft identity platform can be used to secure custom applications that run in Azure and other environments. Although the protocols and pattern descriptions that are also described in this book are applicable to other platforms, the focus in this book is on how to use Azure Active Directory, the Microsoft identity platform, and the OAuth 2.0, OpenID Connect, and MSAL components to secure your applications. It also covers how Azure AD **Business to Consumer** (**B2C**) provides support for securing your consumer-facing applications.

The book provides lots of hands-on and practical demos that you can use as a reference for your own applications. Although the platform evolves rapidly, and new services are added to it frequently, lots of the basics that are described in this book will be applicable for future scenarios as well.

Who this book is for

If you are a developer or architect who has basic knowledge of Azure Active Directory and are looking to gain greater expertise in the application security domain, this is the book for you. In order to learn from this book, you should have knowledge of building web applications and web APIs in C#, and basic Azure knowledge.

What this book covers

Chapter 1, Microsoft Identity Platform Overview, introduces the Microsoft identity platform and gives a high-level overview of the features and capabilities it has to offer. Besides this high-level overview, we also cover the evolution of the Microsoft identity platform as well.

Chapter 2, Azure AD Application Model, focuses on the Azure AD application model and how this is used to sign in users or delegate the sign-in to other identity providers. We dive deep into this by covering all the important parts of the application model for developers.

Chapter 3, Application Types and User Consent, builds upon the previous chapter. We look at the different application types that you can develop and cover user consent. We build a web application that authenticates against Azure AD using our app registration that we registered in the previous chapter.

Chapter 4, The Basics and Evolution of Authentication, takes a step back to look at the basics and evolution of authentication. We examine how authentication has evolved over time into the modern authentication protocols that we are using right now in our applications.

Chapter 5, Securing Applications with OAuth 2.0, OpenID Connect, and MSAL, covers OAuth 2.0, OpenID Connect, and **Microsoft Authentication Library** (**MSAL**) in depth. We finish this chapter by building a secure and modern application using these techniques, protocols, and frameworks.

Chapter 6, Building Secure Services Using the Microsoft Graph API, examines the Microsoft Graph API in depth. We look at the different APIs provided by Microsoft Graph and how to build queries to retrieve data. Lastly, we finish our demo that we started building in the previous chapter and add the functionality to call Microsoft Graph on behalf of the signed-in user.

Chapter 7, Introducing Azure Active Directory B2C, focuses fully on Azure AD B2C. We cover user flows and policies, and set up a web application that authenticates against Azure AD B2C.

Chapter 8, Advanced Features of Azure AD B2C, looks at identity providers in Azure AD B2C, and how you can configure them and add them to your user flows. We cover how you can change the UI of the default Azure AD B2C authentication experience and cover custom domains in Azure AD B2C.

Chapter 9, Azure AD B2C Custom Policies, dives into custom policies and what they can bring to your custom applications. We cover the Identity Experience Framework and create our own custom policy that connects to an Azure function and stored user profile information inside Azure Table storage.

To get the most out of this book

To follow this book, you need to have an active Azure subscription to create an Azure AD and an Azure AD B2C tenant. You also need to have the latest version of Visual Studio or Visual Studio Code installed:

- Visual Studio Code: `https://code.visualstudio.com/`
- Visual Studio: `https://visualstudio.microsoft.com/`

Download the color images

We also provide a PDF file that has color images of the screenshots/diagrams used in this book. You can download it here: `https://static.packt-cdn.com/downloads/9781838646509_ColorImages.pdf`.

Download the example code files

You can download the example code files for this book from GitHub at `https://github.com/PacktPublishing/Azure-Active-Directory-for-Secure-Application-Development`. In case there's an update to the code, it will be updated on the existing GitHub repository.

We also have other code bundles from our rich catalog of books and videos available at `https://github.com/PacktPublishing/`. Check them out!

Conventions used

There are a number of text conventions used throughout this book.

`Code in text`: Indicates code words in text, database table names, folder names, filenames, file extensions, pathnames, dummy URLs, user input, and Twitter handles. Here is an example: "Enter the app package name here, which can be found in the `AndroidManifest.xml` file, then generate and enter the `signature` hash."

A block of code is set as follows:

```
<samlp:AuthnRequest
xmlns:samlp="urn:oasis:names:tc:SAML:2.0:protocol"
xmlns:saml="urn:oasis:names:tc:SAML:2.0:assertion"
ID="ONELOGIN_809707f0030a5d00620c9d9df97f627afe9dcc24"
Version="2.0" ProviderName="SP test" IssueInstant="2014-07-
16T23:52:45Z" Destination="http://idp.example.com/SSOService.
php" ProtocolBinding="urn:oasis:names:tc:SAML:2.0:bindings:HT
TP-POST" AssertionConsumerServiceURL="http://sp.example.com/
demo1/index.php?acs">
```

Bold: Indicates a new term, an important word, or words that you see onscreen. For example, words in menus or dialog boxes appear in the text like this. Here is an example: "From the app registration overview page of the registered application, under **Manage**, select **API permissions**."

> Tips or Important Notes
> Appear like this.

Get in touch

Feedback from our readers is always welcome.

General feedback: If you have questions about any aspect of this book, mention the book title in the subject of your message and email us at `customercare@packtpub.com`.

Errata: Although we have taken every care to ensure the accuracy of our content, mistakes do happen. If you have found a mistake in this book, we would be grateful if you would report this to us. Please visit `www.packtpub.com/support/errata`, selecting your book, clicking on the Errata Submission Form link, and entering the details.

Piracy: If you come across any illegal copies of our works in any form on the internet, we would be grateful if you would provide us with the location address or website name. Please contact us at copyright@packt.com with a link to the material.

If you are interested in becoming an author: If there is a topic that you have expertise in and you are interested in either writing or contributing to a book, please visit authors.packtpub.com.

Share Your Thoughts

Once you've read *Azure Active Directory for Secure Application Development*, we'd love to hear your thoughts! Scan the QR code below to go straight to the Amazon review page for this book and share your feedback.

https://packt.link/r/1838646507

Your review is important to us and the tech community and will help us make sure we're delivering excellent quality content.

Part 1: Getting Started with the Microsoft Identity Platform

In this first part of the book, we focus on what the Microsoft identity platform has to offer developers and how **Azure Active Directory** (**Azure AD**) is key as the underlying service. We look into the Azure AD application model and application types, and get hands-on experience with registering and configuring an application in Azure Active Directory.

This part of the book comprises the following chapters:

- *Chapter 1, Microsoft Identity Platform Overview*
- *Chapter 2, Azure AD Application Model*
- *Chapter 3, Application Types and User Consent*

1
Microsoft Identity Platform Overview

This chapter introduces the first objective in this book, the **Microsoft identity platform**. In this chapter, we will start by introducing the Microsoft identity platform and giving a high-level overview of the features and capabilities it has to offer. As well as the overview, we are also going to cover the evolution of this platform. Then, we are going to dive a bit into the more technical aspects by covering how users are authenticated using the Microsoft identity platform and what the permissions and consent framework is about.

At the end of this chapter, you will have a high-level understanding of the different components that are part of the platform.

The following topics will be covered in this chapter:

- Learning about the Microsoft identity platform
- Understanding the evolution of the Microsoft identity platform
- Introducing Azure Active Directory
- Introducing Azure AD B2B

- Introducing Azure AD B2C
- Setting up an Azure AD tenant
- Adding a user to Azure AD
- Cleaning up the resources

Learning about the Microsoft identity platform

The Microsoft identity platform is a comprehensive set of components that help developers to build applications that sign users in with various types of accounts, such as Microsoft identities or social media accounts. The types of applications that can make use of the platform and its components include web applications, web APIs, and mobile apps.

The Microsoft identity platform components consist of authentication services, a set of open source libraries, and various application management tools. These different sorts of tools are specified in more detail as follows:

- **Industry standards**: The base platform is completely based on industry standards, such as OAuth 2.0, OpenID Connect, and SAML v2.0.
- **Identities**: The platform offers developers the ability to use the OpenID Connect standard-compliant authentication service to authenticate using a variety of identity types:

  - **Work or school accounts**: These are stored in **Azure Active Directory** (**Azure AD**).
  - **Personal Microsoft accounts**: For example, Xbox, Outlook, Skype, and Hotmail accounts.
  - **Social or local accounts**: With Azure AD B2C, you can use both social accounts (such as Facebook, Google, and Twitter) or local (external database or partner email) accounts. Azure App Services authentication supports authenticating using Azure AD and a few social accounts, such as Facebook and Google.

- **Open source libraries**: The Microsoft identity platform offers the **Microsoft Authentication Library** (**MSAL**) and support for other standard-compliant libraries.
- **Application management portal**: Applications can be registered and configured in Azure AD by using the Azure portal. From here, applications can also be configured.

- **Application configuration API and PowerShell**: The Microsoft identity platform has support for registering and configuring your applications using the Graph API and PowerShell. Using this programmatic approach, these tasks can be automated using your *CI/CD pipelines*.

The following diagram illustrates the different components of what the Microsoft identity platform is made of:

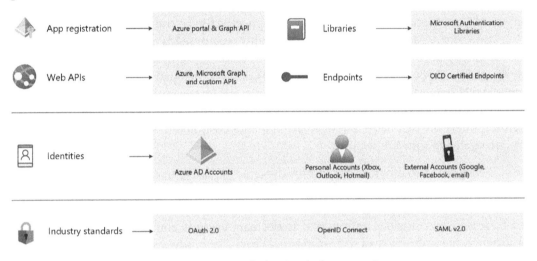

Figure 1.1 – Microsoft identity platform overview

In the next section, we are going to investigate the evolution of the Microsoft identity platform.

Understanding the evolution of the Microsoft identity platform

The Microsoft identity platform is the evolution of the Azure AD developer platform. Many developers have worked with the Azure AD platform previously to authenticate against Azure AD. For this, they have used the **Azure AD v1.0** endpoint to authenticate using only work or school accounts. Work and school accounts are accounts that are all provisioned in Azure AD.

By using the Azure portal, the Microsoft Graph API, and the Azure **AD Authentication Library (ADAL)**, developers can request access tokens from the Azure AD v1.0 endpoint. This can be done for both single-tenant apps as well as for multi-tenant apps.

By using the unified Microsoft identity platform (**v2.0**), you can authenticate using multiple types of accounts. It supports both organizational and consumer accounts to authenticate users. Unlike the v1.0 endpoint, the v2.0 endpoint is capable of authenticating using work or school accounts (that are provisioned in Azure AD), personal accounts, (Outlook, Xbox, Skype, or Live accounts), and social media accounts (for Azure AD **B2C**). Now you only have to write code once and you can authenticate with any Microsoft identity in your application.

You can add the open source MSAL, which is supported for several platforms, such as *.NET*, *JavaScript*, *Java*, and *Python*. Microsoft highly recommends using MSAL to connect to the identity platform endpoints. MSAL is highly reliable and has great performance, is easy to use, has support for **single sign-on** (**SSO**), and is developed using the Microsoft **Secure Development Lifecycle** (**SDL**). SDL is a topic of its own and way beyond the scope of this book, but in short, it is a software development process proposed and used by Microsoft internally that helps to reduce maintenance costs and increases the reliability of software related to software security.

The v2.0 endpoint also provides support for dynamic and incremental consent. This means that instead of specifying all the permissions upfront when you register your app in Azure AD, you can request the permissions incrementally. You only request consent for a basic set of permissions upfront that an ordinary user can consent to themselves. For instance, the ability to read their own profile data. Then, when a user tries to access different data in the application, such as a list of groups in the user's organization, the application will ask for the user or administrator's consent, depending on the permissions and how the tenant is configured. This will be covered in more detail later in this chapter.

MSAL also supports **Azure AD Business to Consumer** (**Azure AD B2C**). Customers that are using your applications and APIs can also use their social accounts to log in to the application.

In the next diagram, you will see an overview of the Microsoft identity experience at a high level, compared to the Azure AD developer platform:

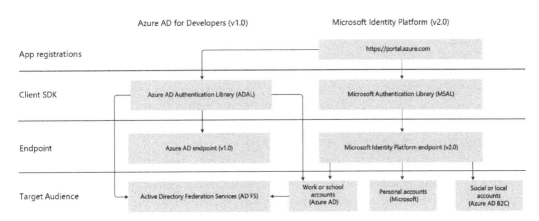

Figure 1.2 – Microsoft identity platform experience

> **Important Note**
>
> MSAL.NET can now directly connect to an ADFS authority. It does not need to go through Azure AD. This is only supported from AD FS 2019 and above. For more information, you can refer to `https://github.com/AzureAD/microsoft-authentication-library-for-dotnet/wiki/ADFS-support`.

Now that we have some background information about the Microsoft identity platform and its predecessor, the Azure AD for Developers platform, we can now dive into Azure AD, which is the backbone for all applications and permissions in Azure.

Introducing Azure AD

Azure AD provides a cloud-based enterprise directory and identity management service. It offers features to give users seamless access to all types of resources, internal and external. For instance, it enables the traditional method of user authentication through a username and password, along with the management of roles and permissions to give users access to a variety of resources and products, such as the Azure portal, applications inside of the corporate network, and also **Software as a Service** (**SaaS**) applications and Office 365.

It offers traditional username and password management as well as roles and permissions management. On top of that, it offers more enterprise-grade features, such as **multi-factor authentication** (**MFA**), and SSO for your applications. It also offers different monitoring and alerting capabilities out of the box.

Azure AD offers different pricing plans, all coming with different types of features and capabilities:

- **Free**: You can gain access to the most basic features by choosing this plan. This consists of support for approximately 500,000 identity objects, seamless SSO, device registration, Azure AD Join, user and group management, external identities with Azure AD B2B, **Pass-Through Authentication** (**PTA**), self-service password change, groups, and standard security reports.

- **Office 365 apps**: This offers no object limit, has an **Service-level Agreement** (**SLA**) for 99.9% uptime, self-service password reset for cloud users, company branding features, and device write-back (a two-way sync for device objects between on-premises directories and Azure).

- **Premium P1**: This offers advanced reporting, MFA and Conditional Access, Advanced Group Access Management, support for the application proxy, which can be used to provides secure remote access to on-premises web applications, **Azure Information Protection** (**AIP**) integration, Microsoft Cloud App Discovery, Azure AD Join, MDM auto-enrollment, and local admin policy customization.

- **Premium P2**: This offers identity protection, **Privileged Identity Management** (**PIM**), access reviews, and entitlement management.

> **Important Note**
>
> For a detailed overview of all the different features for each pricing plan, you can refer to the following site: `https://azure.microsoft.com/en-us/pricing/details/active-directory/`.

Azure AD is also used to manage user identities in **Microsoft 365**. Microsoft 365 is a collection of different services, such as *Windows 10*, *Office 365*, and *Enterprise Mobility*. By default, your Microsoft 365 subscription comes with the free plan of Azure AD, but you can also purchase different plans to get more features.

For developers, Azure AD is primarily used for issuing tokens that enable users to sign in to applications. Before these tokens can be issued, applications need to be registered inside Azure AD, permissions need to be set, and users need to be added that can access the applications or have access to Microsoft 365 data. This is mainly done by IT administrators, but it is also important for developers to know how to put this in place. Developers can also make use of the enterprise-grade security features in Azure AD, such as Conditional Access policies and SSO, for example.

Next to the fact that an Azure AD tenant is created together with your sign-up for an Azure, Microsoft 365, Office 365, or *Intune* account, you can also create an Azure AD tenant manually. An Azure AD tenant is basically a representation of an organization. You create a dedicated instance of Azure AD bound to the organization. It is also possible to create multiple Azure AD tenants. Each Azure AD tenant is completely separated from other Azure AD tenants and has its own work or school identities, Azure AD B2C consumer identities, and app registrations. An app registration can be single-tenant, which only allows authentications from accounts within the tenant where it is registered, or multi-tenant, which allows authentications from all tenants.

In the next sections, we will briefly introduce Azure AD **Business to Business (B2B)** and Azure AD **Business to Consumer (B2C)**.

Introducing Azure AD B2B

This book is focusing on Azure AD from a developer's perspective. This means that, as a developer, you will not work with Azure AD B2B very often, although Microsoft Graph does offer APIs for Azure AD B2B that you can leverage inside your custom applications. You may encounter Azure AD B2B users in the solutions you build.

But, to give a complete overview of the different products and services that Azure AD has to offer, I will give a short introduction to this feature as well.

Azure AD B2B collaboration is a feature on top of Azure AD. You can add external identities to your Azure AD tenant to collaborate with external users inside your organization. Partners or individuals are not required to have an Azure AD or even an IT department. Azure AD B2B uses a simple redemption process to give access to your company resources, Azure environment, or Office 365 environment, using their own credentials. Partners use their own Azure identity management solution with Azure AD B2B. This reduces the administrative overhead that comes with managing accounts with external users. External users can log in to Azure AD-connected apps and services using their own work, school, personal, or social media identities.

Azure AD B2B APIs (using Microsoft Graph) can be used by developers to customize the invitation process or write applications such as self-service sign-up portals. Azure AD External Identities uses a billing model based on **monthly active users (MAU)**, which is basically the same for Azure AD B2C. The first 50,000 users are free, then there is a monthly charge per monthly active user.

Azure AD B2B offers the following features:

- **Management portal**: Azure AD B2B is part of Azure AD, which means that all external users can be managed from the Azure portal. This is fully integrated with Azure AD, and the user experience is completely the same as for internal users.

- **Groups**: You can create groups for external users or add them to dynamic groups. With dynamic groups, administrators can set up rules to populate groups based on user attributes.

- **Conditional Access**: With Conditional Access, you can set conditions for your users. You can enforce external users to use MFA or give them access to certain applications or access from limited locations or devices.

- **Auditing and reporting**: Azure AD B2B is an add-on to Azure AD, which means you can use the auditing ad reporting capabilities that are part of Azure AD. For instance, you can look into the invitation history and acceptance details.

In the next section, we will introduce Azure AD B2C.

Introducing Azure AD B2C

Azure AD B2C is a business-to-customer identity as a service aimed at public-facing mobile and web applications. Customers can use their preferred social, enterprise, or local account identities to get SSO access to your applications and APIs. These applications can be hosted everywhere, in Azure or other cloud providers, but also on-premises.

It offers a set of out-of-the-box authentication providers. These authentication providers can be used in your apps and custom APIs. For this, it uses industry-standard protocols and libraries, such as OAuth 2.0, OpenID Connect, and MSAL.

This means that developers don't have to add additional SDKs for making use of these authentication providers manually to their code; that is all handled by Microsoft and embedded in the SDKs that are used for authenticating against Azure. As well as the authentication providers that are offered by Azure AD B2C, you can also add your own authentication providers.

Azure AD B2C offers the following account types:

- **Social accounts**: Such as Facebook, Google, LinkedIn, and Twitter.

- **Enterprise accounts**: Azure AD accounts, or other accounts that use open standards protocols.

- **Local accounts**: These are accounts using email address/username and password and are registered inside the Azure AD B2C portal.

Your application needs to be registered inside the Azure B2C tenant. After registration, built-in flows and policies can be configured for the app inside the Azure AD B2C portal, where you can enable different authentication providers, set claims, and enable MFA that be used inside your applications. By configuring these user flows inside of the Azure AD B2C portal, they can easily be reused in different types of applications.

> **Important Note**
>
> Azure AD B2C is covered in more detail in *Part 3* of this book: *Azure AD Business to Consumer.*

In the next section, we are going to set up the Azure AD tenant that we are going to use for all the demos in this book.

Setting up an Azure AD tenant

In this section, we are going to set up a new **Azure AD tenant** inside an Azure subscription.

> **Important Note**
>
> If you are new to Azure and don't have a subscription already, you can sign up for a free account here: `https://azure.microsoft.com/en-us/free/`.
>
> Microsoft also offers the Microsoft 365 Developer Program. Here you can sign up for an E5 licensed tenant with no need to sign up for a subscription, no credit card needed, and you get access to sample data packs. The tenant is live by default for 90 days and it will automatically renew if it is actively used. If you want to use an environment that includes a fully functional E5 license including all the features and sample data, this is the way to go. You can sign up for this program here: `https://developer.microsoft.com/en-us/microsoft-365/dev-program`.

To create a new Azure AD tenant, you have to take the following steps:

1. Open a web browser and navigate to `https://portal.azure.com`.

2. In the overview page of Azure AD, in the top menu, select **+ Create a resource**:

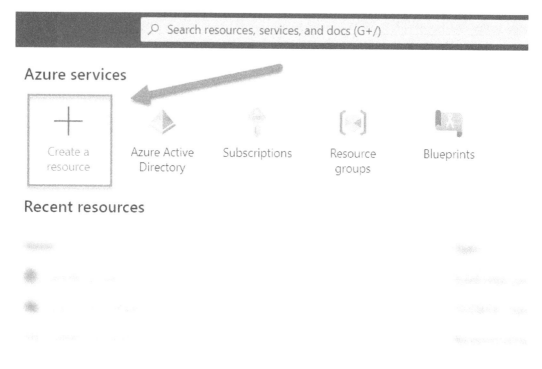

Figure 1.3 – Azure portal overview

3. Search for `Azure Active Directory` in the search box and select it.

4. Click the **Create** button to start creating a new Azure AD tenant.

5. Next, in the **Basic** tab, you need to select the type of tenant that you want to create, an **Azure Active Directory** or **Azure Active Directory (B2C)** tenant. **Azure Active Directory** will be selected by default. Make sure that it is selected and click **Next: Configuration**:

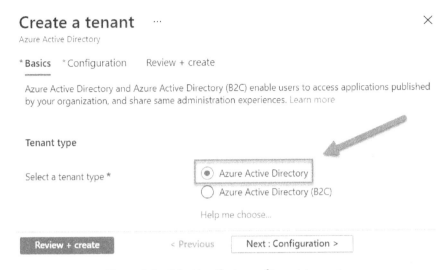

Figure 1.4 – Selecting the type of tenant to create

6. In the next screen, you need to specify the values for the Azure AD tenant. I've used the following values, but you have to fill in a unique name here:

- **Organization name**: `PacktPubDev`.

- **Initial domain name**: `PacktPubDev`. This will result in the following domain name: `PacktPubDev.onmicrosoft.com`.

- **Country/Region**: Here, select your current country or region.

Your settings will look like the following screenshot:

Create a tenant   ...
Azure Active Directory

*Basics   *Configuration   Review + create

Directory details

Configure your new directory

Organization name * ⓘ | PacktPubDev   ✓ |

Initial domain name * ⓘ | PacktPubDev   ✓ |
                                                       PacktPubDev.onmicrosoft.com

Country/Region ⓘ | United States   ⌄ |
                          ✅ Datacenter location - United States
                          Datacenter location is based on the country/region selected above.

Review + create   < Previous   Next : Review + create >

Figure 1.5 – Specifying Azure AD tenant details

7. Click **Review + create** and **Create**. If needed, prove that you are not a robot and then click **Submit** to create the Azure AD tenant.

It will take a couple of minutes before the Azure AD tenant is created. After it is created, we can start adding our first user to it. Let's cover this in the next section.

Adding a user to Azure AD

Now that we have our Azure AD tenant in place, we can add our first user to it. For this, you have to take the following steps:

1. We first need to ensure that the new directory that was created in the previous step is active. For this, we need to select the *directory* icon in the top-right menu, and then select the Azure AD tenant that we have just created:

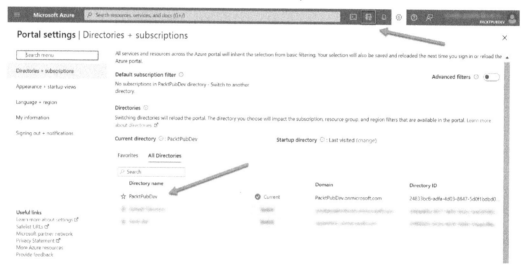

Figure 1.6 – Selecting the new Azure AD tenant

> **Tip**
> If the directory is not yet available in the list, you need to log out and log in again. Then, open the directory menu again and select the directory.

2. Now that we have selected the right directory, we can navigate to the Azure AD tenant.

3. On the **Overview** page of the Azure portal, type `Azure Active Directory` in the top search box and select it. The Azure AD **Overview** page will be displayed.

4. In the left menu, under **Manage**, select **Users**:

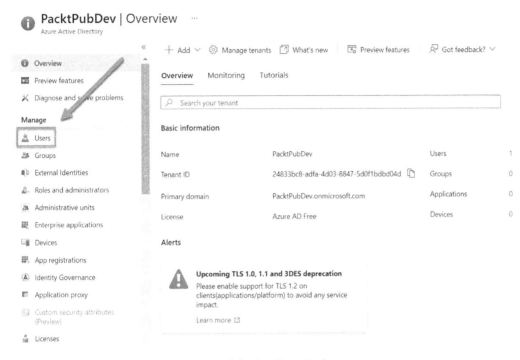

Figure 1.7 – Selecting Users in the menu

5. In the top menu, select + **New user**:

Figure 1.8 – Creating a new user

6. Specify the required values as follows:

- **Username**: `packdemouser1`.

- **Name**: `Packt DemoUser1`.

- **First name**: Packt.

- **Last name**: DemoUser1.

- **Password**: You can choose between letting Azure auto-generate a password or creating your own password. In this case, leave the default value.

This will look like the following screenshot:

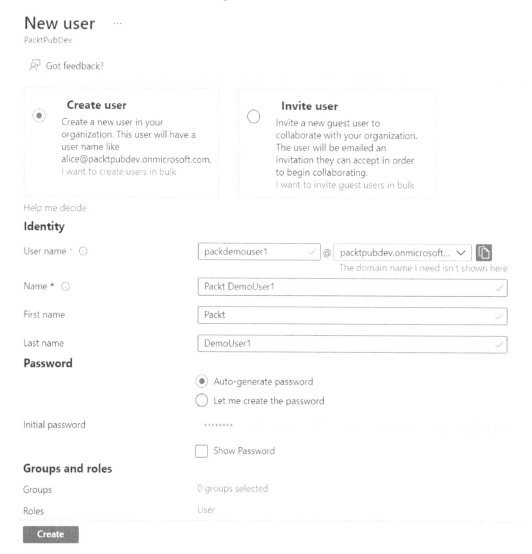

Figure 1.9 – Specifying the user values

7. Click **Create**.

We have now created a new user in our Azure AD tenant. In the next section, we are going to cover how you can delete the Azure AD tenant when it is not needed anymore.

Cleaning up the resources

If you don't intend to continue using the Azure AD tenant, you can easily delete it. If you are planning on using this tenant for the rest of the book, you can skip this part and come back to it when you are ready to delete the tenant.

To delete an Azure AD tenant in the Azure portal, you have to take the following steps:

1. On the **Overview** page of Azure AD, in the top menu, select **Manage tenants**:

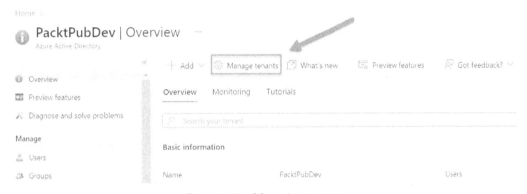

Figure 1.10 – Managing tenants

2. Then, select the Azure AD tenant that you want to delete from the list, and click on **Delete** in the top menu:

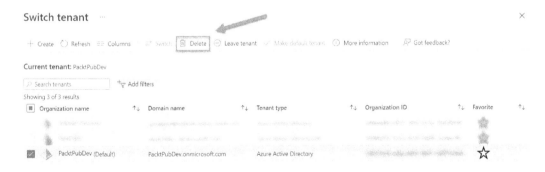

Figure 1.11 – Deleting a tenant

3. Before you can delete the tenant, the users need to be deleted; therefore, under **Required action**, click **Delete all users**:

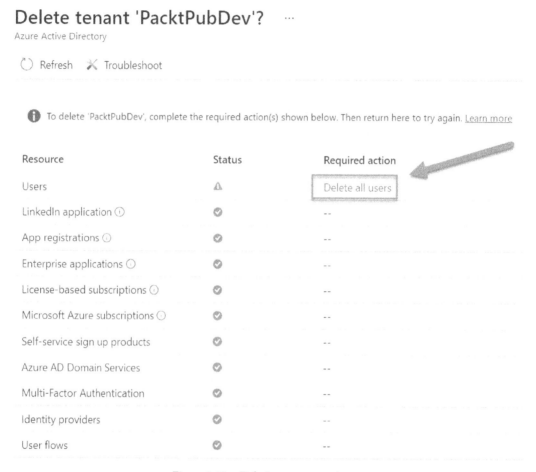

Figure 1.12 – Deleting tenant settings

4. You will be redirected to the **Users** tab where you can delete all the users. Select the users and then in the top menu, click **Delete user**:

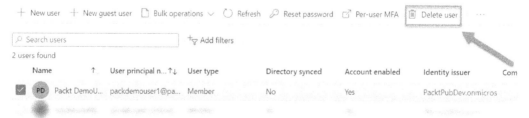

Figure 1.13 – Deleting users

5. Click **OK** when you are asked if you want to delete the selected users.

6. You will notice that the Azure AD administrator cannot be deleted. Navigate back to the Azure AD **Overview** page and click on **Delete tenant** again. Now, you will see that there are no required actions, and you can delete the tenant by clicking the **Delete** button:

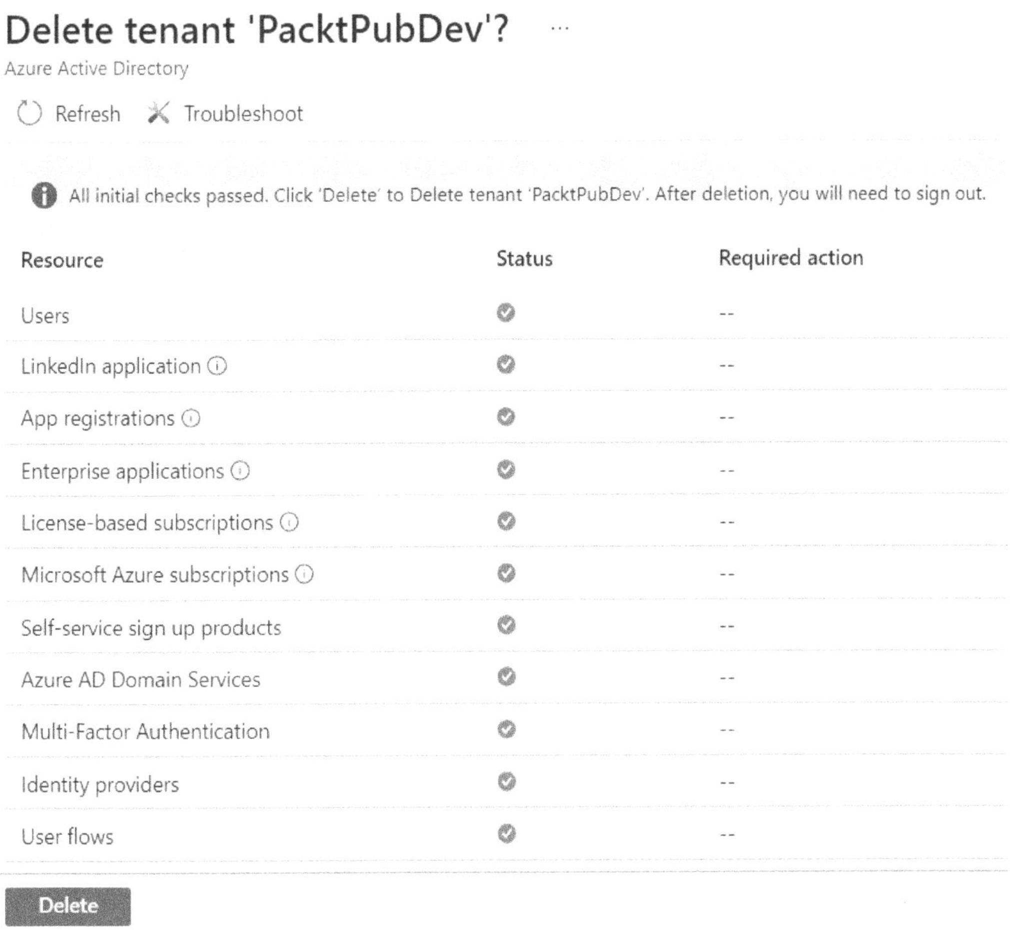

Delete tenant 'PacktPubDev'?   ...

Azure Active Directory

○ Refresh   ✕ Troubleshoot

ⓘ All initial checks passed. Click 'Delete' to Delete tenant 'PacktPubDev'. After deletion, you will need to sign out.

Resource	Status	Required action
Users	✓	--
LinkedIn application ⓘ	✓	--
App registrations ⓘ	✓	--
Enterprise applications ⓘ	✓	--
License-based subscriptions ⓘ	✓	--
Microsoft Azure subscriptions ⓘ	✓	--
Self-service sign up products	✓	--
Azure AD Domain Services	✓	--
Multi-Factor Authentication	✓	--
Identity providers	✓	--
User flows	✓	--

Delete

Figure 1.14 – Deleting an Azure AD tenant

We have now cleaned up our resources by deleting the Azure AD tenant. This concludes this chapter.

Summary

In this chapter, we introduced the Microsoft identity platform. We covered all the different features and capabilities that it has to offer from a high level. Next, we covered Azure AD and the different products that it has to offer. We looked at Azure AD B2B and Azure AD B2C, where the latter is mostly used by developers. Then, we created a new Azure AD tenant in the Azure portal, added our first user to it, and finally, cleaned up our resources and removed the Azure AD tenant.

After this introduction of all the different products and features that are offered by Azure, we are going to focus on registering applications inside our Azure AD tenant in the next chapter.

Further reading

You can check out the following links for more information about the topics that were covered in this chapter:

- *An overview of the Microsoft identity platform*: https://docs.microsoft.com/en-us/azure/active-directory/develop/v2-overview

- *Microsoft Secure Development Lifecycle (SDL)*: https://www.microsoft.com/en-us/securityengineering/sdl

- *External Identities documentation*: https://docs.microsoft.com/en-us/azure/active-directory/external-identities/

2

Azure AD Application Model

In the previous chapter, we introduced the Microsoft identity platform and gave a high-level overview of the different features and capabilities that it has to offer. We covered the evolution of the platform, and briefly covered Azure AD B2B and Azure AD B2C.

In this chapter, we are going to focus on the **Azure AD application model** and how this is used to sign in users or delegate the sign-in to other identity providers. We are going to take a deep dive into this, by covering all the important parts of the application model for developers. We are going to look at single-tenant and multi-tenant apps, cover the redirect URLs and the limitations, and more. We are also going to get some hands-on experience and register an application inside Azure AD.

The following topics will be covered in this chapter:

- Introducing the Azure AD application model
- Learning about application and service principal objects in Azure AD
- Registering an application with the Microsoft identity platform
- Setting redirect URIs
- Understanding permissions and consent
- Understanding certificates and secrets

- Restricting your Azure AD app to a set of users

- Registering an application using PowerShell and the CLI

Technical requirements

To follow this chapter, you need to have an active **Azure AD tenant**. An Azure AD tenant was created in *Chapter 1, Microsoft Identity Platform Overview*. You also need to have the latest version of PowerShell installed on your local system, together with Azure PowerShell: `https://docs.microsoft.com/en-us/powershell/azure/install-az-ps?view=azps-5.4.0`.

Optionally, you can install Windows Terminal. I'm using this for all the demos in this book. For more information about how to install Windows Terminal, you can refer to the following article: `https://docs.microsoft.com/en-us/windows/terminal/get-started`.

Introducing the Azure AD application model

The Azure AD application model is used for signing in users inside of **Microsoft identity**. You can also use the Azure AD application model to delegate the sign-in process to additional identity providers and let them be responsible for this. Adding additional identity providers is a feature that is part of Azure AD B2C.

For an identity provider to know that a user has access to a particular app, the user or the application needs to be registered with the identity provider. Whether it is a web or a mobile application, a web API, or any other application, it needs to be registered to be able to perform identity and access management. By registering the application, you establish a trust relationship between your application and the identity provider, such as the Microsoft identity platform.

As well as signing in users to your application, registering the app with the Microsoft identity platform allows you the following:

- It lets you decide whether you want your users to only sign in using work or school accounts, use personal accounts, or let them sign in using social media accounts using Azure AD B2C.

- You can decide whether you want to let the users sign in only from your organization or other organizations as well. If you only want your users to be able to sign in from your organization, you register a **single-tenant** app. If you want users to sign in from multiple organizations, you register a **multi-tenant** app inside Azure AD.

- Declare a scope, or permissions, your app will use. For instance, you can declare your app will use the `User.Read` scope. When your app runs, it can request permission for your app to read the profile information of the signed-in user. The user, or admin, can then grant your app this scope. While highly recommended, applications do not have to declare the permissions the app will use in the app registration.

- Define your own scopes to define access to your custom APIs. When an application wants access to your custom APIs, it will need to request permissions to the scopes that you define for your web API.

- Customize the branding of the sign-in dialog of your applications. By default, the Azure AD sign-in branding is used. You can adjust this to your organizational branding and make sure that it is in line with the design of the rest of the application.

- Share secrets with the Microsoft identity platform that proves the app's identity. This is relevant in cases where the app is a **confidential client application**. Confidential client applications can store credentials securely. They require a trusted backend server to store the credentials securely.

> **Important Note**
>
> In *Chapter 3, Application Types and User Consent*, we will cover confidential client applications in more detail.

In this section, we have introduced the Azure AD application model. In the next section, we are going to cover application and service principal objects in Azure AD in detail.

Learning about application and service principal objects in Azure AD

When the application is registered in the Azure AD tenant, it will get a unique identifier that is shared with the Microsoft identity platform when it requests tokens. The registered application is called an **application object** inside the Microsoft identity platform. The platform uses the application object to create one or more **service principal(s)**. This service principal represents an application within a specific directory or tenant. When a user signs into a multi-tenant application from a specific tenant, Azure AD creates a service principal, also known as an **enterprise app**, in that tenant. The service principal is used by tenant administrators to control how the application runs in that tenant. The service principal is associated with the application's registration.

Application object

An Azure AD application is defined by its one and only application object. This application object is stored in the home tenant, the Azure AD tenant where the application was registered. It is used as a template to create one or more service principal objects. In every tenant where the application is used, a dedicated service principal object is created. Service principals are not copies of the application object; they each contain different parts of the whole application.

The application object has some static properties applied to it, which is like a class in *object-oriented programming*. You would then try out those properties on all the created service principals (or **application instances**).

Three different aspects of the application object are described when you register the application:

- How Microsoft identity can issue tokens for users to access the application
- The *actions* that the application can take in terms of permissions
- The *resources* that the application might need to access

Service principal object

To access resources that are secured by an Azure AD tenant, the user or the application that requires access must be represented by a security principal. This is the only way that resources can be accessed that are secured by an Azure AD tenant. This applies to both users (user principal) and applications (service principal). This service principal contains the permissions that the application has been granted in a tenant and the conditional access policy for the user or the application in the Azure AD tenant. This will then enable the core features in Azure AD, such as authentication of both the application and the user during sign-in, and the authorization when resources are accessed.

In each tenant where the application is used, there needs to be a service principal created that references the globally unique *app object*. The service principal object then defines what the app can actually do to the specific tenant, who has permissions to access the app, and what resources the app can access. This can be different for each tenant; each tenant may grant only some of the permissions.

When you create or register an application inside of Azure AD using the Azure portal, PowerShell, or the CLI, both the application object and the service principal are created automatically. When you use the Graph API to register the application, you need to first create the application object and then create the service principal as a separate step.

In the next section, we are going to register an application inside Azure AD.

Registering an application with the Microsoft identity platform

In the previous section, we covered the differences between the application object and the service principal. We are now going to put this theory into practice and actually **register an application** inside the Azure AD tenant. For this, we are going to use the Azure AD tenant that we created in the previous chapter.

We are going to register an application using the Azure portal, PowerShell, and the CLI. We will start by registering an app in the Azure portal.

Registering an application using the Azure portal

To register an application using the Azure portal, we have to take the following steps:

1. Open a web browser and navigate to `https://portal.azure.com`.

2. If you have multiple tenants, use the **Directory + subscription** filter in the top-right menu to select the tenant where you want to register the application.

3. On the **Overview** page of Azure, select **Azure Active Directory**, as shown in *Figure 2.1*, or type `Azure Active Directory` in the search box:

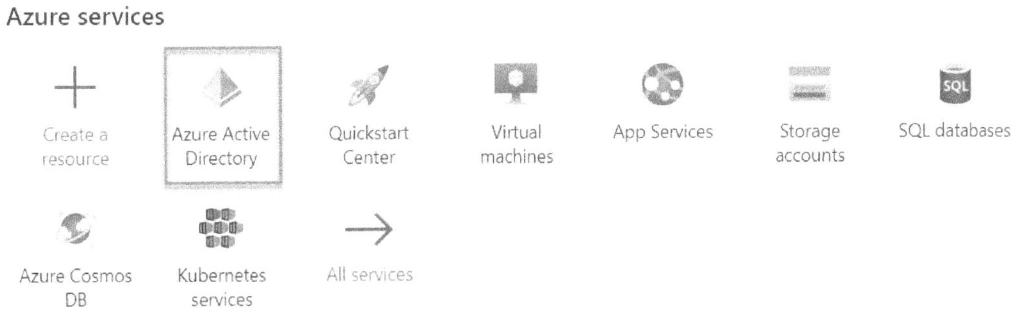

Azure services

Figure 2.1 – Navigating to Azure AD

4. In the left menu, under **Manage**, select **App registrations | New registration**, as shown in the following screenshot:

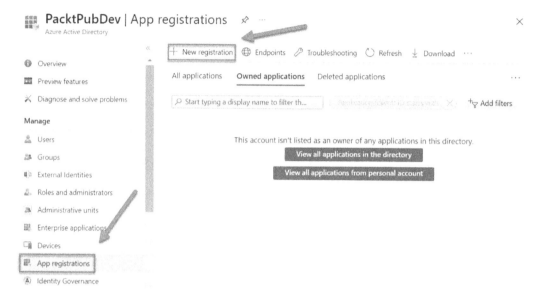

Figure 2.2 – Creating a new app registration

5. In the **App registrations** blade, add the following:

-   **Name**: PacktApp

-   **Supported account types**: Here, you have different options to choose from:

    -   **Accounts in this organizational directory only**, as shown in *Figure 2.3*. Select this option if you want to register a *single-tenant* app (only users or guests in your tenant can use the app).

    -   You can also choose **Accounts in any organizational directory**. Choose this option if you want to register a *multi-tenant* app (if you'd like users from any Azure AD tenant to be able to use your application).

    -   The next option is **Accounts in any organizational directory and personal Microsoft accounts**; choose this one if you want to register a multi-tenant application that can also support users with personal **Microsoft accounts** (**MSA**).

- • The last option to choose from is **Personal Microsoft accounts only**. Select this option if you want to register an app that is only used by users with personal MSA, such as Live, Skype, Xbox, and Hotmail accounts. We are going to pick the first option for this demo: **Accounts in this organizational directory only**.

- • **Redirect URI**: Don't fill in the redirect URI yet, as we are going to configure this in the next section.

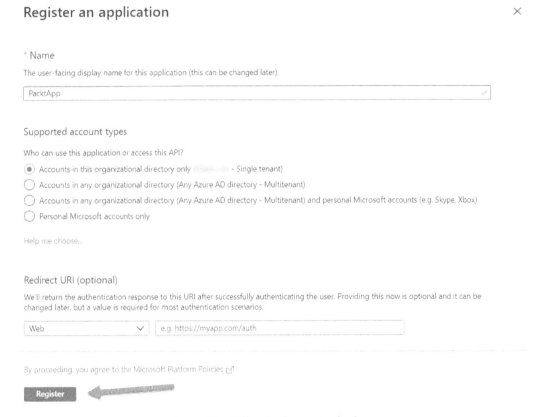

Figure 2.3 – Filling in the required values

6. Select **Register** to register the application inside Azure AD.

7.   When the app is registered, the **Overview** page of the app registration will be displayed. On this Overview page, **Application (client) ID** is displayed. This is the unique value of the application in the Microsoft identity platform and used to access the application from your custom apps, as can be seen in the following screenshot:

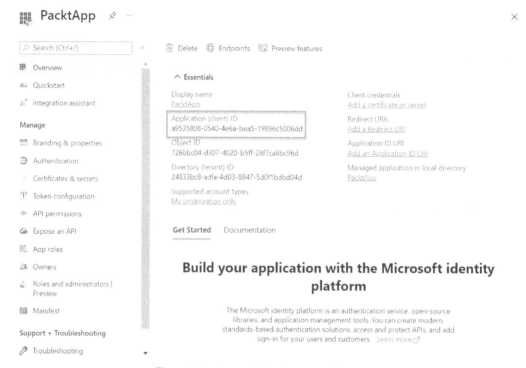

Figure 2.4 – App registrations overview page

Copy the application ID to Notepad, together with the Azure AD tenant ID (displayed below the application ID). We are going to use this, together with the app secret that we are going to generate, later in this chapter. These values will be used in *Chapter 3*, *Application Types and User Consent*, where we are going to build the application.

We have now registered the application using the Azure portal. In the next section, we will take a look at redirect URIs.

Setting redirect URIs

After authentication, the user will be redirected to **Redirect URI** by the Microsoft identity platform. The security tokens will also be sent to this URL. The redirect URI will be a public endpoint in production scenarios, such as `https://packtpub.com/auth-response`. In development scenarios, it's common to also add the endpoint where the app is running locally, such as `https://127.0.0.1/auth-response` or `http://localhost.com/auth-response`.

Redirect URIs can be added or modified inside the Azure portal, using PowerShell and the CLI, or the Graph API. In the Azure portal, the redirect URI is in the platform configuration inside the **App Registration Authentication** settings. For web and single-page applications, it is required to specify the URI manually. For other platforms, such as mobile or desktop applications, you can select a redirect URI that is generated automatically when other settings for the app are configured.

> **Important Note**
> In *Chapter 3, Application Types and User Consent*, we will cover the different types of applications in more detail.

In the next section, we are going to configure a redirect URI in the Azure portal for the app registration.

Configuring the redirect URI

In this demonstration, we are going to **configure the redirect URI** from the Azure portal; therefore, we shall take the following steps:

1. From the app registration overview page, where we finished our previous demo, under **Manage**, select **Authentication**.

2. Under **Platform configurations**, select **+ Add a platform**, as shown in the following screenshot:

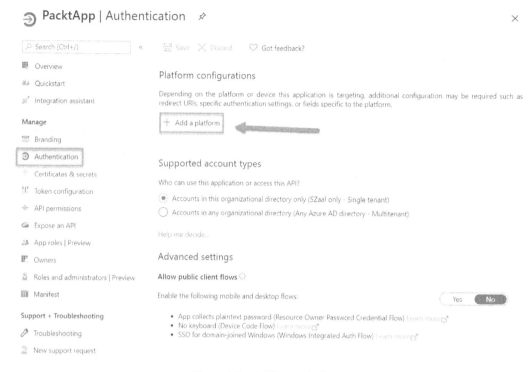

Figure 2.5 – Adding a platform

3. Here, you can choose between the following platforms:

- **Web**: Select this platform for standard web applications. You need to specify a redirect URI manually for your app.

- **Single-page application**: Select this platform if you're building a client-side web app in JavaScript or with a framework such as *Angular*, *Vue.js*, *React.js*, or *Blazor WebAssembly*. You need to specify a redirect URI manually for your app as well.

- **iOS / macOS**: Here, you need to specify the **Bundle ID** found in xcode in `Info.plist` or the build settings. The redirect URI will be generated automatically when the bundle ID is specified.

- **Android**: Enter the app package name here (this can be found in the `AndroidManifest.xml` file) and generate and enter the *Signature* hash. The redirect URI will then be generated automatically.

- **Mobile and desktop applications:** Select this platform for mobile apps that don't use the latest **Microsoft Authentication Library** (**MSAL**) or are not using a broker. Also select this option for desktop applications.

We are manually going to enter the redirect URI. Choose the Web platform:

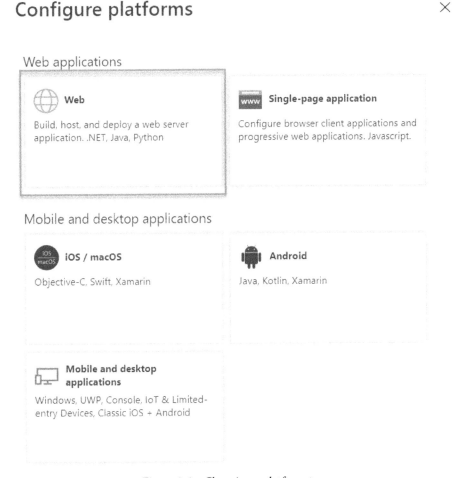

Figure 2.6 – Choosing a platform type

4.   The **Configure Web** page will be displayed. Add the following:

   - **Redirect URIs**: For now, enter `https://localhost.com/auth-response` here. In the next chapter, we are going to focus on building the application. We can then change this URI when we have our app running.

   - Click **Configure**, as shown in the following screenshot:

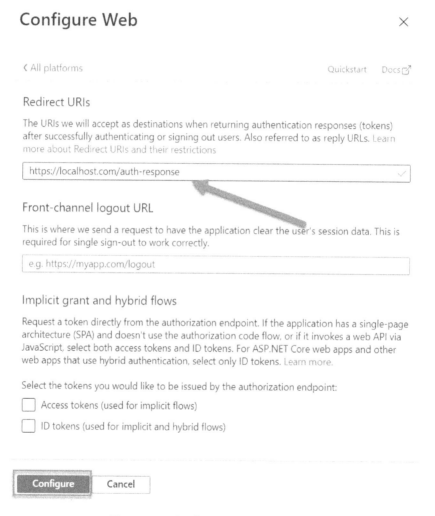

Figure 2.7 – Configuring the redirect URI

We have now configured the redirect URI for the application registration using the Azure portal. In the next section, we are going to cover permissions and consent.

Understanding permissions and consent

The Microsoft identity platform follows an authorization model that gives users and administrators control over how data can be accessed using application registrations.

Let's dive in and look at what they are.

Scopes and permissions

The Microsoft identity platform implements the **OAuth 2.0** authorization protocol. With OAuth 2.0, an app can access web-hosted resources on behalf of a user. Each web-hosted resource that integrates with the Microsoft identity platform has a unique resource identifier, which is called the **Application ID URI**.

For example, here you can see a couple of web-hosted resources with their application ID URIs:

- Microsoft Graph: `https://graph.microsoft.com`
- Azure Key Vault: `https://vault.azure.net`

Third-party web-hosted resources that are registered in Azure AD also have an Application ID URI configured, and for each of these resources, you can also define a set of permissions. With these permissions, you can divide the functionality of that resource into smaller parts. An example of this is **Microsoft Graph**. This is built of a set of APIs, with a set of defined permissions to execute different tasks, such as the following:

- Read a user's profile.
- Write to a user's profile.
- Send an email on behalf of the user.
- Get an overview of all the users that are present in the Azure AD tenant.
- Create a user inside the Azure AD tenant.

Because of this set of defined permissions, the resource has more control over how the API functionality is exposed and has more fine-grained control over its data. A registered application inside the Azure AD tenant can request these permissions from users (**user consent**) and administrators (**administrator consent**). They must approve the request before the application can act on the user's behalf and access data from the service. The difference between whether a user or an administrator must give consent depends on what the API designer configures, how the tenant is configured, and the permission type of the application.

Permission types

The Microsoft identity platform supports two different permission types, **delegated permissions** and **application permissions**. In addition to that, when your registered application makes a request to the target resource, it will then be constrained by **effective permissions**.

In the next section, we are going to cover the differences between the delegated permissions and application permissions that your application is granted, and the effective permissions your application encounters when it makes calls to the target resource.

Delegated permissions

Delegated permissions are used by applications that have a signed-in user. Tasks are executed on the behalf of the user in this case. User consent is given manually when the request is made to the service, either by the signed-in user or by the administrator. Administrators can also grant consent to the application without running the app.

For delegated permissions, the effective permissions of your registered application are the least-privileged intersection of the delegated permissions the app has been granted (by consent) and the privileges of the currently signed-in user. Your app can never have more privileges than the signed-in user.

Examples of these types of requests are as follows:

- An application that reads a user's profile
- An application that writes to a user's profile
- An application that sends an email on behalf of the user

How and when to give this consent will be covered in the next part of this chapter.

Within the Azure AD tenant, the privileges of the signed-in user can be determined by membership, licenses, or policies. For instance, an Office 365 user has certain roles or permissions to access data in the Office 365/Azure AD tenant. On the other hand, **role-based control** in Azure can also give a user certain permissions in the Azure tenant.

As another example, let's say your application has been granted the `User.ReadWrite.All` delegated permission for Microsoft Graph. This permission will grant your application the permission to read and update the user profiles of each user inside the Azure AD tenant. When the request is made to Microsoft Graph, the user signs in and will have these permissions. When the user is a global administrator inside the Azure AD tenant, the application can update all the user profiles inside the tenant. If the user does not have an administrator role inside the tenant, the app can only update the current user's own user profile.

Application permissions

Application permissions are used by applications that run without a signed-in user. These typically belong to applications that require a higher set of permissions, and applications that run in the background, such as *background services* or *daemon apps*. Examples of these types of applications are those that get an overview of all the users that are present in the Azure AD tenant or create a user inside the Azure AD tenant.

For application permissions, the effective permissions are the full level of privileges granted by the permission. For example, your application has been granted the `User.ReadWrite.All` application permission. With this permission, it can update the profile of every user inside the Azure AD tenant.

Now that we have covered scopes and permissions and we have some basic knowledge of the different permission types, we can now configure them inside the Azure portal.

Configuring permissions in the Azure portal

In this demonstration, we are going to configure delegated permissions for the application that we registered in the first demo of this chapter. To configure the permissions, you will need to take the following steps:

1. From the app registration overview page of the registered application, under **Manage**, select **API permissions**.

2. Under **Configured permissions**, you can see that, by default, the application has delegated `User.Read` permissions on Microsoft Graph, which means that the user can sign in and the application can read the user's profile:

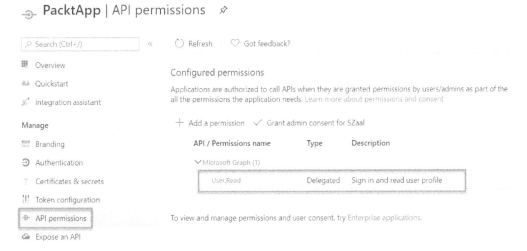

Figure 2.8 – Default permissions

3.   We are going to add some additional permissions to the application. Click on **+ Add a permission**, in the top menu. This will open the **Request API permissions** page where you can select the API to which you want to give your application permission. There are several APIs here to select. We are going to use **Microsoft Graph**, as shown in the following screenshot:

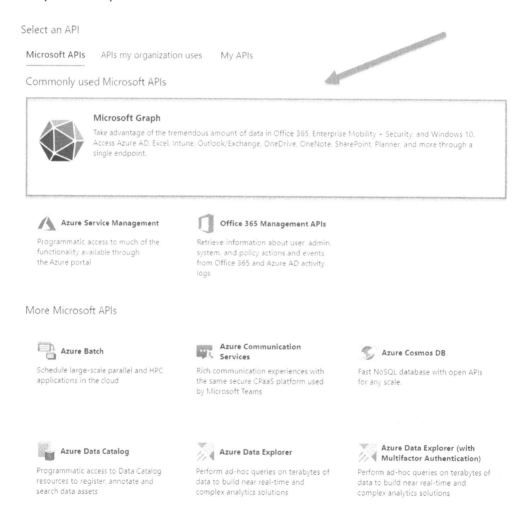

Figure 2.9 – Requesting API permissions

4.   On the next screen, you can choose between delegated permissions or application permissions. Select **Delegated permissions**:

Figure 2.10 – Choosing Delegated permissions

5. This will open the different permission types that you can choose from. For each
    API that Microsoft Graph has to offer, you can configure separate permissions.
    You can also choose some of the **OpenID Connect** scopes here, which are hosted
    on Microsoft Graph as well. Scroll down to the **User** section. Here, select **User.
    ReadWrite**:

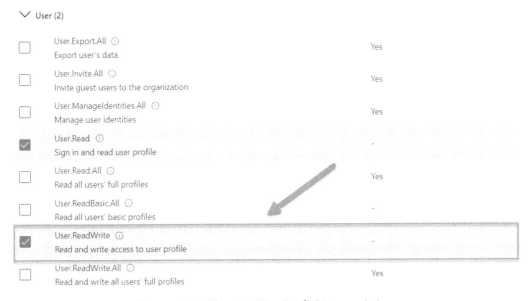

Figure 2.11 – Choosing User.ReadWrite permissions

Important Note

In this example, the goal is to show how you can add additional permissions
to the app registration; however, by using **User.ReadWrite**, you technically
remove the need of **User.Read**. The **User.Read** permission could be replaced
with openid, (which MSAL always adds automatically). **User.Read** gives the
best user experience.

---

6. Click on the **Add permissions** button at the bottom of the screen.

7. You will now see that the permissions are added to the overview page as follows:

Figure 2.12 – Overview of assigned permissions

Now that we have assigned the required delegated permissions to the app, we can proceed with *certificates* and *secrets*.

> **Important Note**
>
> OpenID Connect and Microsoft Graph will be covered in detail in *Part 2* of this book: *Authentication and Protocols*.

Understanding certificates and secrets

There are two types of authentications available for applications inside Azure AD: **application secrets** and **certificate-based authentication**. You need the secret or the certificate to get access to the app registration from your application. Certificate-based authentication is recommended by Microsoft, but for our demonstration, an app secret will do.

In the next demonstration, we are going to configure an app secret.

Configuring an app secret in the Azure portal

In this demonstration, we are going to configure an app secret in the Azure portal. To configure an app secret, we need to take the following steps:

1. From the app registration overview page of the registered application, under **Manage**, select **Certificates & secrets**.

2. Here, you can upload a certificate or you can configure an app secret. Under **Client secrets**, click **+ New client secret**:

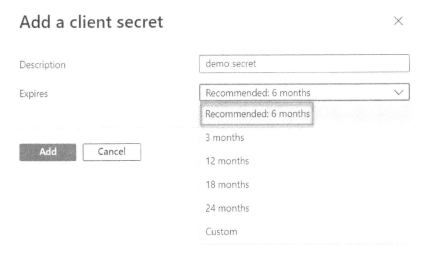

Figure 2.13 – Certificates and secrets

3. Add a description, and choose when you want the secret to expire:

Add a client secret   ✕

Description	demo secret
Expires	Recommended: 6 months ⌄
	Recommended: 6 months
	3 months
	12 months
	18 months
	24 months
	Custom

Add   Cancel

Figure 2.14 – Adding a client secret

4.   Click **Add** to generate the secret.

5.   After generation, immediately copy the secret to Notepad, because it will only be displayed to you once. If you lose the secret, you need to generate a new one:

Figure 2.15 – Generated secret

We have now generated the app secret and copied this to Notepad. Together with the app ID and the Azure AD tenant ID that we copied after registering the application, we are going to use this in *Chapter 3, Application Types and User Consent*, where we are going to build the application.

We have now completed the app registration part and configured all the necessary parts. In the next section, we are going to look at how you can restrict the app to a set of users.

Restricting your Azure AD app to a set of users

When you register an application inside the Azure AD tenant, it is available to all users that authenticate successfully to the tenant. In addition, in the case of registering a multi-tenant app, all users in all the Azure AD tenants where the app is provisioned will have access to the apps by default.

In a lot of scenarios, apps must be restricted to a certain set of users. This can be done easily by adding groups or users to the Enterprise app service principal in Azure AD.

In the next demonstration, we are going to add a user that is already added to Azure AD to the app; therefore, we first need to update the Enterprise app to require user assignment.

Updating the app to require user assignment

First, we need to make some changes to the Enterprise app to require user assignment for it; therefore, we need to take the following steps:

1. In the overview page of Azure, select **Azure Active Directory**.

2. Under **Manage**, select **Enterprise Applications**. You will see your application there in the list. When an application is registered in Azure AD, two types of objects get created: an *application object* and an Enterprise app, or *service principal*. The application object is the one you see under **App Registrations** in Azure AD, which we used to access the app in the previous examples. The service principal is what you see in the **Enterprise applications** blade. Select the application in the list to open the settings as follows:

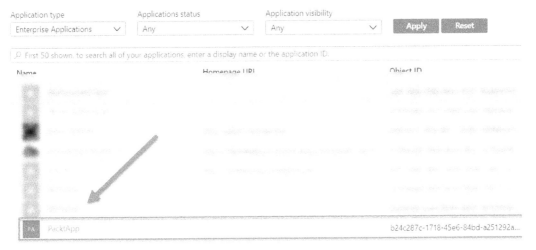

Figure 2.16 – App registration in Enterprise applications blade

3. In the overview blade of the application, under **Manage**, select **Properties**. In the properties, locate the **Assignment required?** setting and set it to `Yes`. When this option is set to `Yes`, users and services that want to access the application must first be assigned to this application, or they won't be able to sign in or obtain an access token:

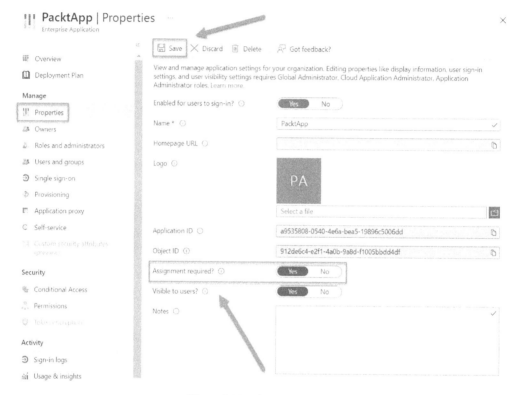

Figure 2.17 – App properties

4. Select **Save**.

In the next section, we are going to assign the app to users and groups.

Assigning the app to users and groups

Now that we have configured the application, we can assign the app to users and groups so they are able to access it. Assigning groups requires Azure AD P1 or P2 licensing. For this, we need to take the following steps:

1. Go to the overview page of the application again in the **Enterprise applications** blade, and in the left menu, select **Manage | Users and groups | + Add user/group** as follows:

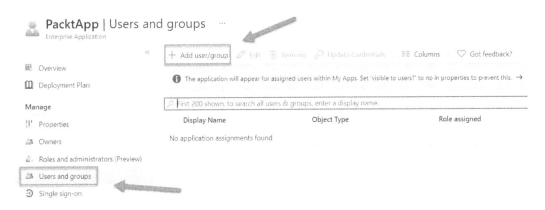

Figure 2.18 – Adding users and groups

2. Under **Users and groups**, click on **None Selected**:

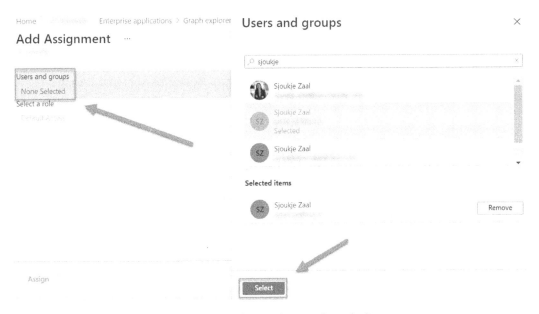

Figure 2.19 – Selecting the user from the list

3. Select the user (or group) that you want to add from the list and click **Select**.

4. The previous blade will be visible again where you need to click **Assign**, which will assign the user to the app:

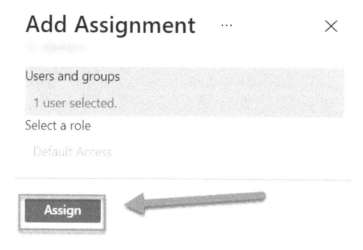

Figure 2.20 – Assigning the user to the app

We have now restricted the application to a set of users in the Azure AD tenant. In the next section, we are going to register and configure an application using PowerShell and the CLI.

Registering an application using PowerShell and the CLI

In the previous sections, we registered and configured the application manually inside the Azure portal; however, the Azure portal is not the only way to register applications in Azure AD. You can also use **PowerShell** or the **CLI** for this. With PowerShell and the CLI, you can register the application programmatically. You can easily register multiple applications this way, and you are able to use these scripts in your **continuous integration and continuous deployment** (CI/CD) pipelines in Azure DevOps, for instance.

In the next demonstration, we are going to register an application using PowerShell.

Registering an application using PowerShell

In this demonstration, we are going to register an application using PowerShell. To register an application, we are going to use **Azure Cloud Shell** in Windows Terminal.

> **Tip**
>
> Instead of connecting via Windows Terminal, you can also use Cloud Shell directly from the Azure portal. If you want more information on how to do this, you can refer to the following article: https://docs.microsoft.com/en-us/azure/cloud-shell/overview.

Connecting to the Azure tenant from Azure Cloud Shell

To use Azure Cloud Shell in Windows Terminal, you need to take the following steps:

1. Open Windows Terminal and select the **Azure Cloud Shell** tab. Here, you can log in to the tenant where you want to register the application. Follow the instructions in Azure Cloud Shell to sign in to the tenant. Once you have signed in, you will see something similar to the following screenshot:

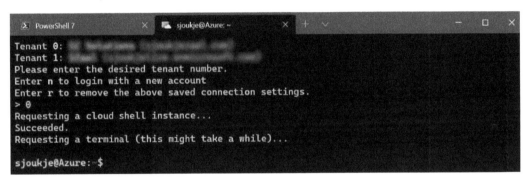

Figure 2.21 – Azure Cloud Shell in Windows Terminal

2. Azure Cloud Shell can be used for PowerShell and the CLI; if you need to switch to PowerShell, type `pwsh`.

Now that we are connected to the right tenant using Azure Cloud Shell, we can register the application.

Registering the application in Azure AD

To register the application using PowerShell, we need to take the following steps:

1. Type the following line of code inside Azure Cloud Shell to register the application:

```
$Application = New-AzADApplication -DisplayName
"PacktPowerShellApp" -IdentifierUris "http://
PacktPowerShellApp"
```

2. The behavior of registering is a bit different when you register the app using PowerShell than registering it using the Azure portal. You need to provide the application ID URI during registration. It's not mandatory to provide this when you register the application in the Azure portal.

3. Next, we need to create and assign a service principal to the application:

    ```
    New-AzADServicePrincipal -ApplicationId $Application.
    AppId
    ```

4. By default, this cmdlet will assign the Contributor role to this service principal, because there are no role and scope parameters defined during creation. For now, this is fine.

We have now registered an application using PowerShell. This can also be done using the CLI. We will do this in the next demo.

Registering an application using the CLI

Registering an application using the CLI can also be done using Azure Cloud Shell. To register the application, we need to take the following steps:

1. To register the application using the CLI, type in the following:

    ```
    az ad app create --display-name PacktCLIApp
    ```

2. In the CLI, it is not mandatory to specify the application ID URI, just as when registering the app using the Azure portal.

3. You do need to create the service principal manually as well. For this, use the following line of code:

    ```
    az ad sp create-for-rbac --name "PacktCLIApp"
    ```

4. This will also create a service principal with the Contributor role assigned to it by default.

We have now registered an application using PowerShell and the CLI. This concludes this chapter.

Summary

In this chapter, we covered application registrations in depth. We focused on application objects and service principals. We also covered redirect URIs for the application registration, looked at permissions and consent, and certificates and secrets. We put the theory into practice and registered an application inside Azure AD and configured it. This application can now be used to build upon in the next chapter.

In the next chapter, we are going to focus on building the actual application that is going to authenticate and connect to our Azure AD application registration.

Further reading

You can check out the following links for more information about the topics that were covered in this chapter:

- *Application and service principal objects in Azure AD*: `https://docs.microsoft.com/en-us/azure/active-directory/develop/app-objects-and-service-principals`

- *Quickstart: Configure a client application to access a web API*: `https://docs.microsoft.com/en-us/azure/active-directory/develop/quickstart-configure-app-access-web-apis`

- *Permissions and consent in the Microsoft identity platform*: `https://docs.microsoft.com/en-us/azure/active-directory/develop/v2-permissions-and-consent`

3
Application Types and User Consent

In the previous chapter, we covered the Azure AD model, including application and service principal objects and how redirect URIs are used. We put that theory into practice and registered an application in Azure AD. Then, we looked at permissions and consent and set the permissions in our app registration process. Finally, we learned how to register an application using PowerShell and the Azure **Command-Line Interface** (**CLI**).

In this chapter, we are going to build on this. First, we are going to look at the different application types that you can develop. We are going to start with the public client and confidential client applications. Then, we are going to look at the different application types. After that, we will build a web application that is going to authenticate against Azure AD by using the app registration process that we registered in the previous chapter.

Next, we are going to cover how Azure AD application consent works in detail. We are also going to learn how to configure consent for an application inside the Azure portal. Finally, we are going to look at publisher verification.

In this chapter, we will cover the following topics:

- Public client and confidential client applications
- Understanding the authorization code flow
- Understanding the different application types
- Building a web app that authenticates users using Azure AD
- Understanding the Azure AD application consent experience
- Understanding how end users consent to applications
- Publisher verification

Technical requirements

To follow this chapter, you will need an active Azure AD tenant – that is, the one you created in *Chapter 1*, *Microsoft Identity Platform Overview*. You will also need to have the latest version of Visual Studio or Visual Studio Code installed:

- Visual Studio Code: `https://code.visualstudio.com/`
- Visual Studio: `https://visualstudio.microsoft.com/`

I'm going to use Visual Studio for the example in this chapter, but you can use Visual Studio Code if you wish.

You can download the source code for this chapter at `https://github.com/PacktPublishing/Azure-Active-Directory-for-Developers/tree/main/Chapter%203`.

Public client and confidential client applications

In the previous chapter, we briefly touched on **confidential client applications**. In this chapter, we are going to cover them in more depth.

Public client and confidential client applications are part of the *OAuth 2.0* framework. Applications can either be confidential or public. The main difference is that a confidential application can hold credentials (such as the client ID and client secret) securely. We will cover this in more detail in the following subsections.

Confidential client applications

Confidential client applications can store credentials securely. They are typically run on servers and are considered difficult to access because they run in a secure environment. For that reason, they can keep a secret. They are capable of holding configuration-time secrets and each instance has a distinct configuration, which includes the client ID and client secret. The client ID and client secret are stored securely and can be accessed by the application at runtime. Examples of confidential client applications include web apps, web API apps (only when they call another API), and service/daemon apps. Web applications are the most common types of confidential client applications. The client ID is exposed through the web browser, but the secret is kept secret and passed only in the backchannel and never exposed to users directly.

Public client applications

Public client applications are apps that run in a web browser, on desktops, or on devices. They are not capable of, nor trusted to, safely store application secrets. These applications only access web APIs on behalf of the user and only support public client flows. Public client applications don't have client secrets because they cannot hold configuration-time secrets.

Public client and confidential client apps have similarities and differences:

- They both maintain a token cache and can acquire tokens silently. The main difference here is that confidential client apps also have an app token cache for tokens that are used only for the app itself. One thing to note here is that confidential client tokens are not user tokens.

- Both types of applications can manage user accounts and they can get an account from the user token cache or its identifier, and they can remove an account as well. However, mixing app and user tokens in the same app should be avoided. This means that the app decides which users can do what.

- Confidential client applications have three different ways to acquire a token. Besides that, they have one way to compute the URL of the identity provider's authorization endpoint. Public client applications have four different ways to acquire a token (four different authentication flows).

Note

In *Chapter 5, Securing Applications with OAuth 2.0, OpenID Connect, and MSAL*, we will learn how **Microsoft Authentication Library** (**MSAL**) acquires and caches tokens in more detail.

In the upcoming sections of this chapter, we are going to build different types of applications. We will look at confidential client applications and public client applications and how you can build them. We will start by looking at the basic **sign-in flows**.

Understanding the authorization code flow

Before we dive into the code, some basics around application sign-in flows need to be covered. As we have mentioned in the previous chapters, the Microsoft identity platform supports authentication for different types of application architectures. All these architectures are fully based on industry standards, such as *OAuth 2.0* and *OpenID Connect*. On top of that, Microsoft has released a set of client libraries that can be used inside your applications to authenticate identities and acquire tokens to access protected APIs. These libraries are part of the MSAL.

> **Important Note**
> OAuth 2.0, OpenID Connect, and MSAL are covered in detail in *Part 2* of this book.

Multiple types of flows are supported in OAuth 2.0 and OpenID Connect, as well as the Microsoft identity platform. In *Chapter 5, Securing Applications with OAuth 2.0, OpenID Connect, and MSAL*, we will cover them in more detail. In this chapter, we want to cover the most used flow and the flow that we are going to use for our demo later in this chapter. The flow that we are going to cover in this chapter is the **authorization code flow**, which will be described in the next section.

Authorization code flow

For web applications, the sign-in flow is as follows:

1. The flow starts with the client application directing the user to the /authorize endpoint. The user will click on a sign-in button to start the flow.

2. Then, the user authenticates using one of the configured login options and may receive a consent page, listing the permissions that the Microsoft identity platform will provide to the application.

3. After authenticating successfully, the Microsoft identity platform will redirect the user to the application and provide an authorization code.

4. The application will send the authorization code to the Microsoft identity platform, including the application's client ID and client secret.

5. The information that's provided will be validated by the Microsoft identity platform. After successful validation, the access token and the refresh token will be returned.

6. The application can use the access token to send a request to the web API to gain access to the secured data and information.

7. The token is validated by the web API.

8. The data is returned to the application.

9. After a short period, the token will expire. The application will send the refresh token, including the application's client ID and client secret.

10. A new access token is returned to the application.

11. The application will use the new access token to call the web API (and the data will be returned).

The following diagram displays the interaction between the web app and the web API:

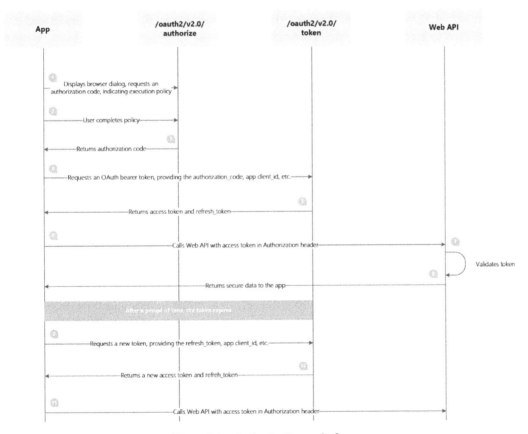

Figure 3.1 – Authorization code flow

Now that we have covered the authorization code flow, we are going to briefly look at the different application types.

Understanding the different application types

In this section, we are going to cover the different *application types* and some examples of use cases where these application types are used.

Single-page applications

Single-page applications (**SPAs**) are used in many modern web application scenarios. Many modern web applications are built as client-side SPAs and are written in languages such as JavaScript or SPA frameworks such as Angular, Vue, and React. These applications have different authentication requirements than the traditional server-side web applications because they run on a web browser.

The Microsoft identity platform offers two different options for SAPs to sign users in and retrieve tokens to access the web APIs or backend services:

- **OAuth 2.0 Authorization Code Flow** (with **PKCE**): By using the authorization code flow, applications are allowed to exchange an authorization code for ID tokens, which represent the authenticated user, and access tokens to call protected APIs. This flow also returns refresh tokens that can be used to get long-term access on behalf of the user, without the need to interact with the user. By using refresh tokens, the user will not be bothered to sign in again after the original token expires. **Proof Key for Code Exchange** (**PKCE**) is an extension of the authorization code flow that allows the user to securely perform the OAuth exchange from public clients and prevents several attacks. This was originally designed to protect mobile apps but proved to be useful for every OAuth client, including web apps that use a client secret. It can prevent authorization code injection.

- **OAuth 2.0 Implicit Flow**: This flow is similar to the OAuth 2.0 authorization code flow (with PKCE); it allows the application to retrieve an ID and access tokens. However, the implicit grant flow does not return a *refresh* token. This flow is only recommended as part of a hybrid flow. For other scenarios, this is no longer a suitable authentication method because third-party cookies are removed from browsers in the process.

> **Important Note**
>
> In *Chapter 5, Securing Applications with OAuth 2.0, OpenID Connect, and MSAL*, we will cover the different OAuth flows in more depth. This also includes the flow described here.

In the next section, we will cover web apps and web APIs.

Web apps and web APIs

Web apps authenticate users in a browser. Most APIs do not authenticate the user; they use the access token provided when the API is called by a web app. The user arrives at the API pre-authenticated. There are multiple scenarios; there are web apps that sign in users directly, web apps that call web APIs that need authentication, scenarios where web APIs need to be protected, and web APIs that call other web APIs. Let's look at the flows that are used for these different scenarios in more depth:

- **Web Apps That Sign In Users**: This scenario uses the web browser to authenticate the user. The web app directs the user's browser to sign them into Azure AD. Azure AD will return the token, which contains claims about the user in a security token. This scenario uses the OpenID Connect standard protocol, which can be simplified using middleware libraries.

- **Web Apps That Call Web APIs**: This scenario assumes that you have already completed the steps for web apps that sign in users. This type of application is a confidential client application; you need to register a secret application password or certificate in Azure AD. This secret is then passed on during the call to Azure AD to acquire a token.

- **Protected Web API**: In this scenario, your app registration must expose at least one **scope** or **application role**. Scopes are used in cases where the web APIs are called on behalf of a user. Application roles are exposed by web APIs known as **deamon apps** (applications that call web APIs on their behalf). When you create a new web API registration, choose the correct token version for your API. For modern web APIs, this value is 2. This will support both work or school accounts, as well as personal Microsoft accounts. Legacy APIs can also use the *null* token version. This will only support organizational accounts (work and school).

- **Web APIs That Call Web APIs**: Here, an application (this can be a SPA, web, desktop, or mobile application) will send a request to a protected web API. In the authorization header, it will pass on a bearer token, which is also called a **JSON Web Token (JWT)**. This token will be validated by the web API and will use the MSAL to request another token from the Microsoft identity platform (Azure AD) so that the protected web API can call the second web API on behalf of the user.

In the next section, we are going to cover **desktop apps**.

Desktop apps

When you build desktop apps, you will run into cases where you want to sign users into your applications and call web APIs. Examples of APIs include different Microsoft APIs, such as *Microsoft Graph*, your own protected APIs, and other third-party APIs. For this, there are several options:

- **Interactive Token Acquisition**: There are different ways to acquire tokens by interacting with the user – that is, if your desktop application supports graphical controls (Windows form, WPF, and macOS applications), if your **.NET Core** application is authenticating to Azure AD using the system browser, or if your application is a **Node.js Electron** application that runs in a Chromium instance.

- **Silent Token Acquisition**: Windows - hosted applications that are joined to Azure AD or running on computers that are joined to a Windows domain can acquire a token silently by using **Windows Integrated Authentication**.

- **Username and Password**: Although this method is not recommended, you can use a username and password in public client applications. Using this method can introduce several constraints to your application. For example, you cannot sign in users who need to perform **multi-factor authentication** (**MFA**), and you cannot benefit from **single sign-on** (**SSO**). This method is only provided for legacy reasons because it is against the principles of modern authentication.

- **Portable Command-Line Tools**: When you're building portable command-line tools, such as a .NET Core application running on Linux or Mac, and you accept that the authentication will be delegated to the system browser, you can use interactive authentication. .NET Core uses the system's browser for authentication because it doesn't provide a web browser. When you don't want the authentication to be delegated to the system browser, you can use the device code flow. This flow is used for applications that don't have a browser, such as IoT applications.

> **Important Note**
>
> In *Chapter 5, Securing Applications with OAuth 2.0, OpenID Connect, and MSAL*, we will cover the different OAuth flows in more depth, including the device code flow.

In the next section, we are going to cover **deamon apps**.

Deamon apps

Deamon apps are used in cases where web APIs are called on behalf of themselves, and not on behalf of a user. Some examples of use cases for deamon apps include *desktop* or *web* applications that are performing batch operations. Web applications are used to provision users to a directory or web APIs that manipulate directories and not users.

Typically, users cannot interact with deamon apps; the app requires its own identity. This means that all the required API permissions need to be configured at the application registration level. Incremental consent at the user level is not possible in these cases and is also not supported.

There are also common cases where a **non-deamon** application needs to use client credentials, even when they act on behalf of a user, such as when secrets need to be accessed from an **Azure SQL Database** or **Azure Key Vault**. In this case, they need to access a resource under their own identities.

Other examples of applications that acquire tokens for their own identities are as follows:

- **Applications That Have Registered a Client Secret in Azure AD**: This can be an application password or certificate. This secret is then passed to Azure AD during the call to retrieve a token.

- **Client Confidential Apps**: These apps access resources independently of users and need to prove their identity. These applications also need to be approved in Azure AD by administrators.

In the final subsection, we are going to cover **mobile apps**.

Mobile apps

For mobile applications, it is important to provide a seamless and personalized user experience. Mobile developers can use the Microsoft identity platform to provide this to Android and iOS users. Mobile applications can sign in to Azure AD, Azure AD B2C, and can use personal Microsoft accounts to sign in. They can also acquire tokens to call web APIs on behalf of these users. For this, they use MSAL. MSAL implements the **OAuth 2.0 authorization code flow**.

There are a couple of design and architecture choices for mobile apps that need to be considered:

- **Implement SSO**: SSO is enabled through the Microsoft identity platform and MSAL. This can be enabled through the device's browser or the *Microsoft Authenticator* (for Android, you can use the Intune Company Portal).

- **Support Different User Configurations**: Many mobile users need to comply with device-compliance policies or conditional access policies. All these scenarios need to be supported when you're building a mobile app.

- **User Experience**: The user experience is essential for mobile apps as it allows users to see the value of the app before you require them to sign in. It's important that you only ask them for the required permissions, nothing more.

- **Implement Shared Device Mode**: This mode supports shared-device scenarios, such as in retail, hospitals, manufacturing, and finance.

> **Important Note**
>
> Shared device mode is beyond the scope of this book. If you are building mobile apps and want more information about this, you can refer to the following website: `https://docs.microsoft.com/en-us/azure/active-directory/develop/msal-shared-devices`.

Now that we understand the different flows and application types, we can put this theory into practice. In the next section, we are going to build our first application.

Building a web app that authenticates users using Azure AD

In this section, we are going to learn how to build an **ASP.NET Core** application that is going to authenticate against Azure AD. We are going to implement the **web apps** that the *sign in users* scenario described in the previous section.

The demo follows this flow:

Figure 3.2 – Sign-in flow

You can download the source code from this book's GitHub repository as a starting point. We are going to walk through the authentication code and use Visual Studio for this example.

We are also going to use the app registration that we created in the previous chapter. For this demonstration, we are going to use **PacktCLIApp**. After registering the application, we copied the *app ID*, *app secret*, and *tenant ID* to **Notepad**. We are going to use these values here. But before we can build the application, we need to register the **redirect URIs** and make sure that the right permissions have been set. We are going to do this in the Azure portal.

Configuring redirect URIs and setting the right permissions

In this section, we are going to configure the redirect URIs for the ASP.NET Core web application for our app registration process. Follow these steps:

1. Open a web browser and navigate to `https://portal.azure.com`.

2. If you have multiple tenants, use the **Directory + subscription** filter at the top right to select the tenant where you want to register the application.

3. In the overview page of Azure, select **Azure Active Directory** or type `Azure Active Directory` in the search box.

4. From the left menu, under **Manage**, select **App registrations**.

5. Locate the **PacktCLIApp** application that we registered in the previous chapter. Click on the display name of the app:

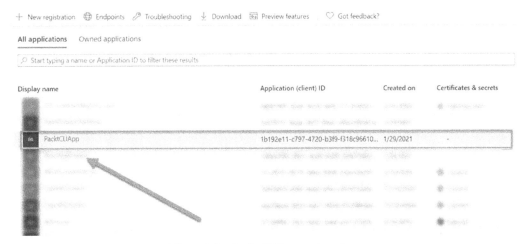

Figure 3.3 – PacktCLIApp registration

6. On the **App registrations** settings page, from the left menu, select **Authentication**. There, under **Platform configurations**, click on **+ Add a platform**:

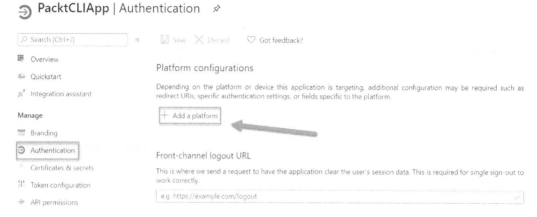

Figure 3.4 – Adding a platform

7. Next, select the **Web** application platform:

Figure 3.5 – The Web application platform

8. On the next screen, set `https://localhost:44321/` as the redirect URI and click **Configure**:

Figure 3.6 – Adding the first redirect URI

9. Now, we need to add another redirect URI. You can do this on the **Authentication** overview page by clicking on **Add URI** under **Web**:

Figure 3.7 – Adding the second redirect URI

10. Here, add the `https://localhost:44321/signin-oidc` URI. This URI is needed for ASP.NET Core applications. The `/signin-oidc` endpoint is how you can return to your application to complete the sign-in process of the OpenID Connect authentication flow.

11. Click the **Save** button at the top of the page:

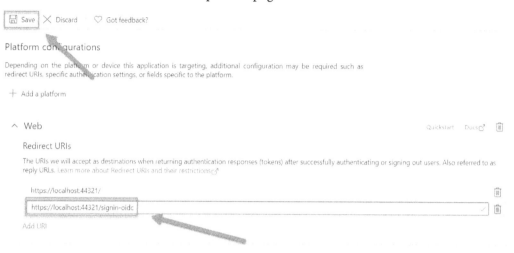

Figure 3.8 – Adding the /signin-oidc endpoint

12. Finally, we need to configure the **front-channel logout URL**. This is part of OpenID Connect and is a mechanism for notifying concerned relying parties that an end user has been logged out of the identity provider. It submits the notification as a **special logout token** (JWT) that is posted directly to the relying party. On the **Authentication** overview page, under **Front-channel logout URL**, add `https://localhost:44321/signout-callback-oidc`. Click **Save** at the top of the page.

13. On the new page that opens, under **Implicit grant and hybrid flows**, enable **ID tokens**. This example requires the ID token to be enabled to sign the user in. Click **Save** at the top of the page:

Implicit grant and hybrid flows

Request a token directly from the authorization endpoint. If the application has a single-page architecture (SPA) and doesn't use the authorization code flow, or if it invokes a web API via JavaScript, select both access tokens and ID tokens. For ASP.NET Core web apps and other web apps that use hybrid authentication, select only ID tokens. Learn more.

Select the tokens you would like to be issued by the authorization endpoint:

☐ Access tokens (used for implicit flows)

☑ ID tokens (used for implicit and hybrid flows)

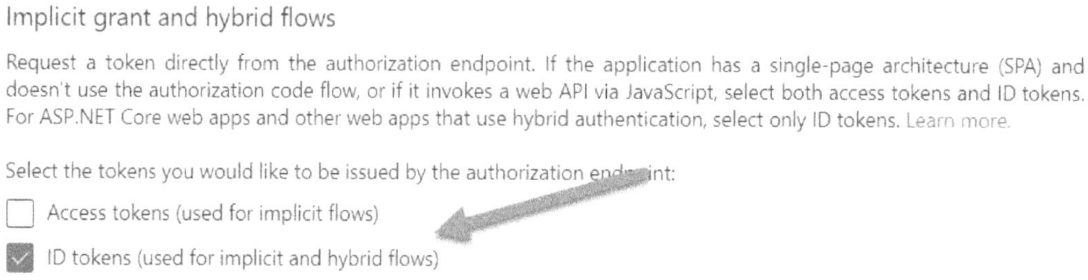

Figure 3.9 – Enabling ID tokens

14. Now that the URIs have been set, we need to add the required permissions. From the left menu, select **API permissions**. Then, at the top of the page, click **+ Add a permission**. Select **Microsoft Graph** and click **Delegated permissions**. Then, scroll down to the **User** tab and select **User.Read** permissions:

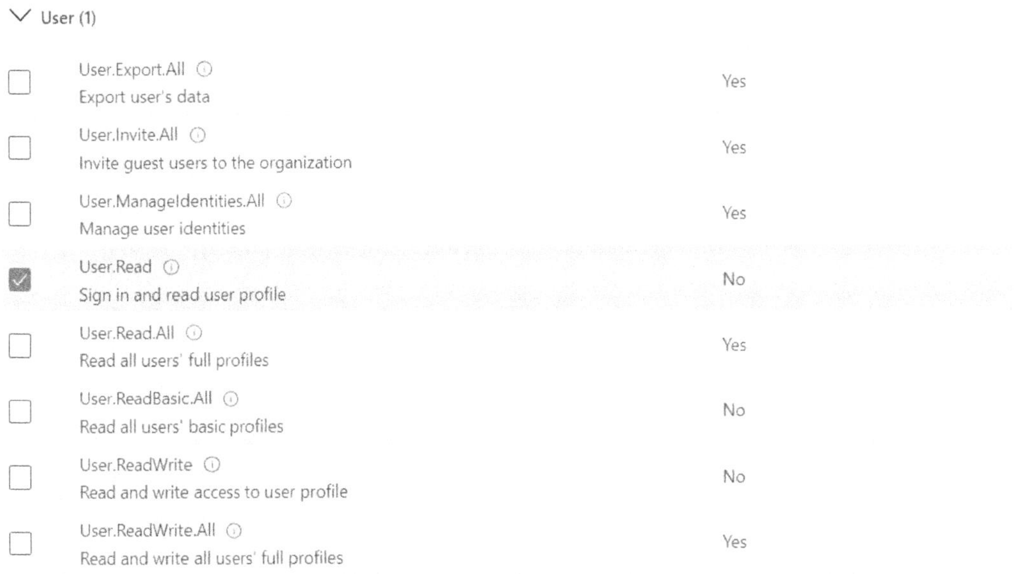

⌄ User (1)

☐   User.Export.All ⓘ
     Export user's data   Yes

☐   User.Invite.All ⓘ
     Invite guest users to the organization   Yes

☐   User.ManageIdentities.All ⓘ
     Manage user identities   Yes

☑   User.Read ⓘ
     Sign in and read user profile   No

☐   User.Read.All ⓘ
     Read all users' full profiles   Yes

☐   User.ReadBasic.All ⓘ
     Read all users' basic profiles   No

☐   User.ReadWrite ⓘ
     Read and write access to user profile   No

☐   User.ReadWrite.All ⓘ
     Read and write all users' full profiles   Yes

Figure 3.10 – Selecting the necessary permissions

15. Finally, click **Add permissions**.

With that, we have configured the redirect URIs for the application and set the required permissions. In the next section, we will start building the application.

Building the application

In this section, we are going to build the application. We are not going to build this application from scratch because we want to focus on the authentication part of it, and not on building the actual application. Therefore, we are going to use the application from this book's GitHub repository. We will configure its settings so that it connects the application to Azure AD and look at the .NET Core authentication code.

To set up the application, follow these steps:

1. First, we need to download the application from GitHub. Download the application and open it in Visual Studio or Visual Studio Code. I'm going to use Visual Studio for this example.

2. First, we are going to make some changes to the `appsettings.json` file so that we can connect to the app registration in Azure AD. We copied the domain, tenant ID, and client ID when we registered the app in the previous chapter. If you forgot to copy this, you can obtain these values again from the Azure portal. Open the `appsettings.json` file and replace the following values:

    •   **Domain**: Enter the domain of your tenant; for example, `yourdomain.onmicrosoft.com`.

    •   **TenantID**: Enter the ID of the tenant. This can be retrieved from the Azure portal. From the **App registrations** blade, select **Endpoints** and use the GUID in any of the URLs.

    •   **ClientID**: Enter the application ID that you obtained from the Azure portal.

3. Once you have filled in these values, the `appsettings.json` file will look as follows:

```json
{
    "AzureAd": {
        "Instance": "https://login.microsoftonline.com/",
        "Domain": "            .onmicrosoft.com",
        "TenantId": "233f4bcb-a            ",
        "ClientId": "bef3c69e-1            ",
        "CallbackPath": "/signin-oidc",
        "SignedOutCallbackPath ": "/signout-callback-oidc"
    },
    "Logging": {
        "LogLevel": {
            "Default": "Information",
            "Microsoft": "Warning",
            "Microsoft.Hosting.Lifetime": "Information"
        }
    },
    "AllowedHosts": "*"
}
```

Figure 3.11 – appsettings.json example

4. Open `Startup.cs` and verify that the `Microsoft.Identity.Web` NuGet package has been added to the project. This package controls how users sign in and access the service. It is used to simplify the sign-in process and retrieve a token.

5. In the **ConfigureServices** method, comment out the following lines:

```
services.AddAuthentication(OpenIdConnectDefaults..
AuthenticationScheme)
```

```
.AddMicrosoftIdentityWebApp(Configuration.
GetSection("AzureAd"));
```

6. Then, uncomment the following line:

```
services.
AddMicrosoftIdentityWebAppAuthentication(Configuration);
```

7. This will enable the application to use the Microsoft identity platform endpoint, which is capable of signing users in with both *work* and *school* accounts and *personal* Microsoft accounts.

8. Next, open the launchSettings.json file and ensure that the application URL is set to http://localhost:44321 and that sslPort is set to 44321.

9. This demo application does not have a custom dedicated **Account Controller** to handle sign-in and sign-out requests. The Microsoft.Identity.Web. UI library has a built-in Account Controller for you that you can use in your applications. Under the previous line of code in the Startup.cs class, ensure that the following method has been added:

```
services.AddControllersWithViews(options =>
        {
            var policy = new
AuthorizationPolicyBuilder()
                .RequireAuthenticatedUser()
                .Build();
            options.Filters.Add(new
AuthorizeFilter(policy));
        });
        services.AddRazorPages()
            .AddMicrosoftIdentityUI();
```

10. In ASP.NET Core, the sign-in button is exposed in Views\Shared_ LoginPartial.cshtml (for an MVC app). It is only displayed when the user is not authenticated: it is displayed when the user has not signed in or out yet. The **sign out** button is displayed when the user is already signed in. The Account Controller is defined in an area named MicrosoftIdentity, in the Microsoft.Identity.Web.UI NuGet package. Open the Views/Shared/_ LoginPartial.cshtml file and ensure that the asp-area tag is set to asp-area="MicrosoftIdentity".

11. Build the solution and run it. If necessary, accept the *IIS Express SSL certificate*. Once the web browser has loaded, you will be redirected to the identity platform endpoint (`https://login.microsoftonline.com/`). Sign in using your *work* or *school* account or *personal* Microsoft account:

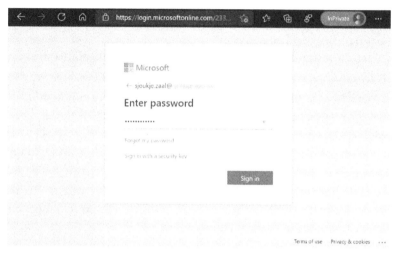

Figure 3.12 – Sign- in page

12. The first time you run this application, you will be asked to give consent to let the application act on your behalf (this will be covered in more detail in the next section):

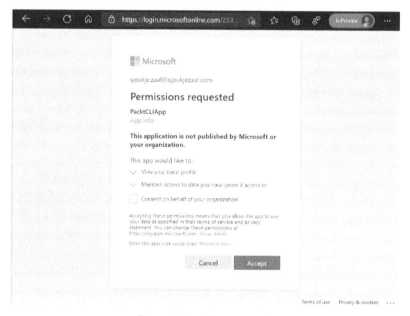

Figure 3.13 – User consent

13. Click **Accept**; you will be redirected to the web app. We configured this redirect URL in the Azure portal in *Step 1*. This redirect will contain the token and the claims in the header of the response. You will be signed into the application, as shown in the top menu bar. Here, you will see the email address that you used to sign into the application. You will also see the **Sign out** button, which is displayed when the user is signed in:

Figure 3.14 – Signed into the web app

14. Close the web app.

In this section, we registered the required configurations, set permissions in the Azure portal, and built a web app that uses Azure AD to authenticate the user. We also granted the application permission to act on the user's behalf. In the next section, we are going to look at the consent experience in Azure AD.

Understanding the Azure AD application consent experience

Applications that are registered inside Azure AD and are integrated with the Microsoft identity platform can be accessed by end users using various accounts, such as their work or school accounts. Using these accounts, applications can access the data from your organization where they have been granted permission.

Before the application can access the data, an end user or tenant admin must grant the application permissions to do so. Different permissions allow different levels of access, as we covered in the previous chapter. The actual user experience of granting consent will differ, depending on the policies that have been set on the user's Azure AD tenant, the role that the user has inside the tenant, and the permissions that are being requested by the application.

This means that both **tenant administrators** and **application developers** have some control over the consent experience of the end user. Administrators can set and disable policies inside the Azure AD tenant, while application developers can set the types of permissions that are being requested and can set if they want to guide users through the user consent flow or the admin consent flow:

- **User Consent Flow**: Using this type of flow, an application developer directs users to the authorization endpoint where the user only gives consent to the current user.

- **Admin Consent Flow**: Here, the application developer directs users to the admin consent endpoint, where an admin user needs to give consent for the whole tenant. To ensure that the admin consent workflow will work properly, all the permissions should be listed in the `RequiredResourceAccess` property in the application manifest.

> **Important Note**
>
> For more information about the application manifest, please refer to the following article: `https://docs.microsoft.com/en-us/azure/active-directory/develop/reference-app-manifest`.

The consent prompt that is presented to the user when an application requests a token contains all the required information for users to determine whether they trust the application to access that data. The consent prompt looks as follows:

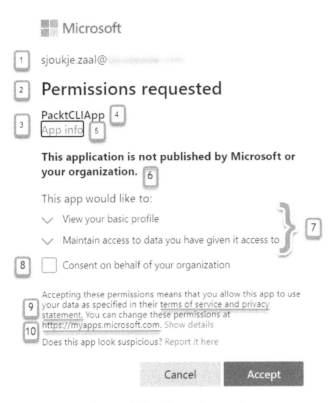

Figure 3.15 – Consent prompt

Let's look at the highlighted points in more detail:

1. **User identifier**: The user that is signing into the application.

2. **Title**: When the user is going through the user consent flow, the title will be
   Permissions requested. When the user is going through the admin consent flow,
   the title will have an additional line: **Accept for your organization**.

3. **App logo**: This image is provided by the application developers and will be the app's
   logo or icon.

4. **App name**: This is the name of the application and is provided by the application
   developers as well.

5. **Publisher domain**: This should be the configured domain that ownership is validated by. This is also provided by the application developer. This can be evaluated for trustworthiness by the user.

6. **Publisher information**: This specifies whether the application has been published by your organization or by Microsoft.

7. **Permissions**: This list contains the permissions that are being requested by the client application. These permissions should always be validated by the user so that they understand which data is requested. Application developers should request access to the permissions with the least privileges.

8. **Consent**: Here, you give consent on behalf of your organization.

9. **App terms**: These terms contain links to the terms of service and the privacy statement of the application. The publisher of the application is responsible for outlining the rules in their terms of service. Additionally, the publisher is responsible for disclosing the way they use and share the data in their privacy statement.

10. **Link**: Here, a link to `https://myapps.microsoft.com` will be displayed. By navigating to that link, users can review and remove any non-Microsoft applications that currently have access to their data.

With that, we have covered the Azure AD application consent experience. In the next section, we are going to cover how to configure how **end users** consent to applications.

Understanding how end users consent to applications

You can configure how end users consent to applications that you register inside Azure AD. Azure AD offers app consent policies for this that you can set for your apps. These policies describe the conditions that must be met before an app can be consented to. You can set policies with conditions for the app that is requesting access.

You can set limits on when the end users are allowed to grant consent to your applications by configuring the app consent policy in the Azure portal. You can also set policies to define when your apps need to request administrator review and approval.

There are four different types of consent settings:

- **Do not allow user consent**: With this setting enabled, your end users can't grant permissions to applications. The users can continue to sign into applications that they previously consented to, or that have been consented to by an administrator. They will not be able to consent to new permissions or apps. However, if the user has been granted a directory role using **role-based access control** (**RBAC**) that includes the permission to grant consent, the user will be able to consent to new apps.

- **Allow user consent for apps from verified publishers, for selected permissions**: Users can only consent to apps that are registered in your tenant or published by a verified publisher. To select which permissions users are allowed to consent to, you must classify the permissions.

- **Allow user consent for apps**: By enabling this setting, all users will be allowed to consent to any permissions that don't require administrator consent for the application.

- **Custom app consent policy**: You can also create custom app consent policies to gain even more control over the conditions.

Now that we have a basic understanding of the different options you can choose from to configure consent for your application, let's configure these settings in the Azure portal.

Configuring how end users consent to applications

In this section, we are going to configure app consent for the application that we registered in the previous chapter, and which we used for our application. Follow these steps:

1. Open a web browser and navigate to `https://portal.azure.com`.

2. If you have multiple tenants, use the **Directory + subscription filter** option at the top right to select the tenant where you want to register the application.

3. On the overview page of Azure, select **Azure Active Directory** or type `Azure Active Directory` in the search box.

4. On the **Azure Active Directory** overview page, under **Manage**, select **Enterprise applications**.

5. On the **Enterprise applications** overview page, under **Security**, select **Consent and permissions**:

6. Here, you can choose whether you want to allow users to give consent for apps (which is the default value). You can also configure that only administrators can give consent for applications. For this, you have to select the setting shown in the following screenshot:

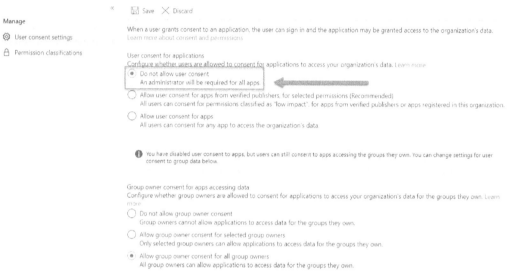

Figure 3.16 – Consent and permissions

7. Click **Save** to enable this setting. By enabling this, end users are not allowed to give consent; only administrators can.

In this section, we learned how to configure and influence the consent process from an application management perspective. There are a lot of additional configuration settings and possibilities you can set, but those are beyond the scope of this book. I highly recommend that developers building applications that use the Microsoft identity platform for authentication learn more about this. For more information about the different features, go to the official Microsoft documentation for application management: `https://docs.microsoft.com/en-us/azure/active-directory/manage-apps/`.

In the next and last section of this chapter, we are going to look at **publisher verification**.

Publisher verification

Before users allow your application to access their data, and before companies add your application to their tenant, there is one very important prerequisite: they should trust your application to do this.

With publisher verification, you can prove that your application integrates with the Microsoft identity platform and is built by authentic application developers. By doing this, the administrators and end users of your application can safely trust your app.

When the application is marked as publisher verified, this means that the publisher of the application has verified their identity using a **Microsoft Partner Network** (**MPN**) account. The verification process is completed by the publisher, and they must associate their MPN account with their application registration. After the verification process, a blue *verified* badge will appear on the Azure AD consent prompt and other screens.

This feature is primarily for developers that are building multi-tenant applications and are leveraging the industry-standard framework and authentication libraries, such as OAuth 2.0 and OpenID Connect, together with the Microsoft identity platform. These applications can request access to data coming from the Microsoft Graph APIs, or sign in users using OpenID Connect.

This has the following benefits for the administrators and end users of your applications:

- **Increased Transparency and Risk Reduction for Customers**: Customers can understand which applications are published by developers they trust. Then, they can securely use these applications inside their organization.

- **Smoother Enterprise Adoption**: Administrators can configure *user consent policies* and use the publisher verification status as one of the primary policy criteria.

- **Improved Branding**: When the user is presented with the Azure AD consent prompt, a *verified* badge will appear. This badge will also appear on the enterprise apps page, and additional UX surfaces are used by admins and end users.

For applications that use OAuth2.0 to request permissions that go beyond basic sign-in, reading user profiles, and requesting consent from users in different tenants than the one the app is registered in, becoming a verified publisher is strongly recommended. For these applications, a warning will be displayed on the consent screen, where the user will be informed that the application that they are using is coming from unverified publishers and is risky. Lack of a verified publisher means that your app may require admin consent much more often but will still work when consent is granted.

There are a couple of requirements that need to be fulfilled for you to become a verified publisher:

- First, you need an MPN ID for a valid Microsoft Partner Network account. This account needs to complete the verification process and needs to be a **Partner Global Account (PGA)** for your organization.

- Your application needs to be registered inside an Azure AD tenant and needs to have a configured **Publisher Domain**.

- The user that is responsible for verifying the application needs to be authorized to make changes to the MPN account in Partner Center and the app registration process in Azure AD. In Azure AD, the user needs to be a member of either the **Global Admin**, **Cloud Application Admin**, or **Application Admin** role. In Partner Center, the user must have either the **Global Admin** (this is a shared role that's mastered in Azure AD), **MPN Admin**, or **Accounts Admin** role.

- The user that is responsible for verifying the application must sign in using MFA.

- The publisher must agree with the Microsoft identity platform for developers' *Terms of Use*.

> **Important Note**
> Configuring a publisher domain for your application is beyond the scope of this book. If you want more information on how to configure this, please refer to the following article: `https://docs.microsoft.com/en-us/azure/active-directory/develop/howto-configure-publisher-domain`.

Now, let's summarize this chapter.

Summary

In this chapter, we looked at the public client and confidential client applications. We covered the different application types and how to build a web application that authenticates against Azure AD using an app registration. In the second part of this chapter, we looked at Azure AD application consent in more detail, together with publisher verification. This has given you a solid foundation regarding the different application types that can be integrated with Azure AD. We will use this foundation in the upcoming chapters to build applications that have been secured with Azure AD.

In the next chapter, we are going to take a step back and look at the basics and evolution of authentication. We are going to cover how authentication has evolved, specifically in OAuth 2.0, which is the standard in Azure AD. We are also going to cover the differences between first-generation authentication protocols and modern authentication protocols.

Further reading

Check out the following links for more information about the topics that were covered in this chapter:

- *Application management documentation*: `https://docs.microsoft.com/en-us/azure/active-directory/manage-apps/`
- *How to configure an application's publisher domain*: `https://docs.microsoft.com/en-us/azure/active-directory/develop/howto-configure-publisher-domain`

Part 2: Authentication and Protocols

In this second part, we cover authentication in depth. We look into the different authentication protocols, along with diving into how to secure applications using OAuth 2.0, OpenID Connect, and MSAL. Lastly, we examine one of the core services of Azure, the Microsoft Graph API.

This part of the book comprises the following chapters:

- *Chapter 4, The Basics and Evolution of Authentication*
- *Chapter 5, Securing Applications with OAuth 2.0, OpenID Connect, and MSAL*
- *Chapter 6, Building Secure Services Using the Microsoft Graph API*

4
The Basics and Evolution of Authentication

In the previous chapter, we covered the different application types that can use Azure AD for authentication and looked at user consent. We covered public client and confidential client applications, how application sign-in flows work and the different application types, such as web apps and APIs, deamon apps, and more. Next, we built a web app that authenticates users using Azure AD. Finally, we covered how users consent to applications and looked at publisher verification.

In this chapter, we are going to take a step back and look at the basics and evolution of authentication. This chapter will not contain code samples; instead, it will look at how authentication has evolved into the modern authentication protocols that we are using right now in our applications.

We will start this chapter by explaining how identity protocols evolved. After that, we will look at the difference between authentication and authorization. Then, we will go back in time and cover pre-claims authentication techniques. Here, we will cover claims-based identity and first-generation protocols. Finally, we are going to cover modern protocols.

In this chapter, we are going to cover the following topics:

- Evolution of identity protocols
- Authentication versus authorization
- Pre-claims authentication techniques
- Claims-based identity
- First-generation protocols
- Modern protocols

Evolution of identity protocols

In this chapter, we are going to cover how authentication has evolved, the different authentication protocols that were used in the past, and what we are using now. Not much code is going to be shown in this chapter, but for newcomers in the identity field, this will give you some more context about how we got here, what the shortcomings are of older technologies, and how we got to where we are now.

The identity landscape, as we currently know it, is the result of a couple of decades of protocols and technologies evolving to address the needs of application architectures.

Older technologies, such as passwords and integrated authentication, still play a key role in enabling modern scenarios such as SSO from a mobile application or accessing an OAuth 2.0-protected web API in Azure AD.

Many of the protocols and standards that are going to be covered in this chapter are still heavily used in the market. For this reason, it is important to cover them here. However, these are older protocols that are not used in modern authentication anymore.

In the next section, we are going to look at the difference between authentication and authorization.

Authentication versus authorization

Before we dive into how authentication evolved over the past few decades and the different protocols, there is one basic topic that needs to be covered: the difference between authentication and authorization.

Both terms are often used in combination with security, especially when it comes to gaining access to a system. Although they are both heavily related, they are very different. There is a huge difference between gaining successful entry to an application (**authentication**) and what you are allowed to do once you are inside (**authorization**).

In the next few sections, we are going to cover both terms in more detail.

Authentication

Authentication means confirming your identity. It is the process of proving that you are who you say you are (this is sometimes shortened to **AuthN**). To verify the identity of the user, the system obtains some credentials to verify the user. If the credentials that are provided by the user (or system or application) are valid, the authorization process will start. In many cases, the authentication process will happen alongside the authorization process.

Authentication is handled in the Microsoft identity platform by using the OpenID Connect protocol. Azure AD also supports SAML and WS-Federation for authentication for older applications.

> **Note**
> OpenID Connect will be covered in more detail in *Chapter 5, Securing Applications with OAuth 2.0, OpenID Connect, and MSAL.*

Authorization

Authorization is the process of granting an authenticated party (such as a user, system, or application) permission to do something. It controls access to specific data and defines what to do with that data (this is sometimes shortened to **AuthZ**). Once a user has been authenticated to the system, the next step is to determine what resources can be accessed by the authenticated user.

Authorization is handled in the Microsoft identity platform by using the OAuth 2.0 protocol. However, technically, the Microsoft identity platform only authorizes applications. It has no technical ability to authorize users. This is simple for application permissions where only the application is involved. In cases where users are present, delegated permissions must be configured. In this case, both the application and the user need to be authorized. The Microsoft identity platform provides authorization for apps via permissions and consent. It provides key information that's required to authorize the user – that is, the user's identity that is in the access token. The resource (protected API) needs to have that user identity and authorize the user on its own.

> **Note**
>
> OAuth 2.0 will be covered in more detail in *Chapter 5, Securing Applications with OAuth 2.0, OpenID Connect, and MSAL.*

In the next section, we are going to learn how the Microsoft identity platform handles authentication and authorization, as well as what services it has to offer for this.

Authentication and authorization using the Microsoft identity platform

The Microsoft identity platform offers different protocols and services for implementing authentication and authorization in your application, resources, and solutions:

- **Authentication**: For authentication, both Azure AD and the Microsoft identity platform make use of industry standards, such as OAuth 2.0 and OpenID Connect, as well as SAML and WS-Federation. Because OpenID Connect is built on top of OAuth 2.0, it uses the same flows and terminologies.

- **Authorization**: For authorization, both Azure **Role-Based Access Control** (**RBAC**) and API permissions are used. RBAC provides fine-grained access management for Azure resources. This authorization system is built on Azure Resource Manager, which is the control plane for everything in Azure.

In *Chapter 3, Application Types and User Consent*, we briefly discussed permissions and consent. With OAuth 2.0, an app can access web-hosted resources on behalf of a user. Each web-hosted resource that integrates with the Microsoft identity platform has a unique resource, called an app registration resource. In Azure AD, an API needs a unique application ID URI; the permissions are covered by specifying the API permissions for an app registration. You need to define scopes for delegated permissions and app roles for the application-allowed member type for application permissions. These permissions will be returned in the access token.

For other Azure services and resources, such as Azure Key Vault, Azure Storage services, different databases, and so on, you can ensure that the application is allowed full access to the Azure resource on behalf of the signed-in user using RBAC. However, the level of access that the user has inside the Azure service (reading, contributing, or admin permissions, for instance) is defined by configuring the roles in RBAC in Azure.

Now that we have covered the differences between authentication and authorization and how this is implemented in the Microsoft identity platform, we are going to cover some different pre-claims authentication techniques.

Pre-claims authentication techniques

Pre-claims authentication techniques are the basics of authentication. Although these techniques are still heavily used in the identity landscape nowadays, they are old techniques, and frankly not secure enough anymore. In this section, we are going to cover password-based authentication and integrated authentication and look at the flaws of these authentication methods.

Password-based authentication

Throughout history, passwords have been used to verify someone's identity. In ancient Rome, watchwords were required for soldiers to enter certain areas. These watchwords were changed every day, engraved into tablets, and shared among the soldier units.

Passwords have also been used with computers since the earliest days of computing. The first computer system that implemented password login was the **Compatible Time-Sharing System** (**CTSS**), an operating system that was introduced at MIT in 1961. CTSS had a login command that requested a user password.

Authentication is the process of verifying who a user claims to be. If we look at authentication, three factors can be used: **something you know**, **something you have**, and **something you are**. Something you know could be a password, or some other personal information, such as your mother's maiden name. Something you have could be a physical item, such as a smartphone or FIDO key. Finally, something you are is referring to biometric data, such as a fingerprint, retina scan, and so on.

Password-based authentication falls into the **something you know** category and is still the most common form of authentication. Even nowadays, every time you sign up for an app or website, you are mostly going to be asked to create a username and a password to identify yourself. This password will then be stored in an encrypted form in the database. This username and password will be linked to the user profile and to the different attributes that make up the identity.

For an application, a user is a set of different attributes that are relevant to the functionality that it provides. Applications use these attributes to drive the experience and behavior. Some examples of attributes include date of birth, shipping address, email address, and so on. All these attributes make up the identity of the user; based on this identity, the application will act in a certain way. These attributes are then stored in a dedicated user profile store. Based on the user profile, the application can fetch certain data for the user, load a profile, store orders for a particular user, show advertisements or recommended content, and more.

Passwords are still heavily used in the identity space. Developers are still implementing username and password user-store systems. The reason behind this is that this is relatively easy to implement and that they have complete control over the relationship between the user and the application. Also, there are still a lot of libraries in different programming languages that support this kind of authentication.

However, it is not a good idea to only use username and password authentication anymore. It dramatically increases the risk of unauthorized access to applications, data, and information. Because almost every application or service uses usernames and passwords for authentication, people often reuse the same password for different services. This way, it is easier for them to remember. This means that if the password of one service gets into the wrong hands, unauthorized people can get access to not only that service, but also to other services where the user has used the same password. Another issue is that people often use weak passwords because they are easier to remember. Password cracking tools are getting good at guessing these easy-to-remember passwords and we see a lot of stories in the news that organizations' password databases have been hacked. This happens even more than we notice as a lot of attacks never get detected by anyone.

In the next section, we are going to look at integrated authentication in more detail.

Integrated authentication

Back in the 90s, many businesses were starting to implement local networks and connect their computers to them. Before that, developers mostly implemented authentication for every application independently. This exposed a lot of limitations, in particular for users in a work environment. It was not very useful for storing the work profile of the user in multiple databases separately for each application. It was also not possible to keep that all in sync correctly. It was not very productive for users either because they needed to sign in with different credentials in each application that they used for their daily work.

In 1999, Microsoft Active Directory was released. Active Directory allowed developers to migrate users' profiles, storage, and credentials from each application to a centralized solution that was connected to the local network of the organization. The employees signed in when they got to their workstation and started their working day. Once they had done that, this resulted in automatic authentication and they had access to all the applications that were connected to the network. Using this approach, not only do the employees exist on the network, but all the entities need to authenticate to the system. This includes computers, servers, and more.

The **Domain Controller** (**DC**), a central server, plays a crucial role in this approach. This dedicated server is responsible for storing all the artifacts that make up a user's or system's identity and it is also responsible for setting up communication between the different entities that reside in a network. This was, and still is, an effective form of authentication in a trusted and local network. Administrators can manage identities, access, and policies from a central place and applications can focus on business processes without having to worry about authentication. Finally, users have a consistent user experience and don't need to provide credentials each time they shift between the different applications that they use.

Now that we have covered some pre-claims authentication techniques, which are still used in a lot of scenarios, let's look at claims-based identity.

Claims-based identity

Each organization is part of an ecosystem that includes customers, suppliers, partners, and more. They need to collaborate with other companies. After successfully implementing local networks and Active Directory (and other equivalent tools and products) to centralize identities, access, and security, the need arose for organizations to connect with the networks of other organizations.

Local networks and intranets were not suitable for these needs. Organizations could have well-implemented and managed intranets, but the domain controllers were unable to connect to each other. Besides that, a new trend appeared where applications were hosted off-premises by hosting providers and, later, cloud providers. This further exposed the limits of an approach based entirely on local networks.

In scenarios where apps were hosted at different places, such as external data centers and cloud providers, business apps still needed to have access to the full identity of the user to work properly. To address these needs, a new industry standard was needed. This resulted in the birth of claims-based identity. Claims-based identity is not an actual protocol; it is a set of concepts that are implemented in other protocols.

What are claims?

Earlier in this chapter, we discussed that a user's identity is made up of a set of attributes, such as a given name, gender, address, email address, and so on. A **claim** is such an attribute, but it's added to an authentication token. This token is the envelope that contains different claims about a user and is a collection of different claims. The following claims can be part of the token:

- User ID or username

- Email address

- Phone number

- Nationality

- Membership in different security groups

These claims can be used by different systems that support claims-based authentication and describe the user from different aspects. This can't be achieved with username and password authentication.

How claims-based identity works

Claims-based identity is a common and shared way for applications to retrieve identity information they need for a user inside their organization, other organizations, and on the internet.

Claims-based authentication allows users to authenticate on external systems. The claims are packaged and signed into an authentication token and sent by an issuer or **Identity Provider** (**IdP**) to party applications through a **Security Token Service** (**STS**). The package is transmitted using an industry-standard method, such as SOAP, JWT, or **Security Assertion Markup Language** (**SAML**). This ensures that the claims share the same format across different authentication sources and applications. Because the token is signed, it cannot be tampered with; otherwise, its signature will be broken.

The STS is an external system that acts as the issuing authority. It validates the incoming credentials, creates a secure token with the claims in it, and then returns this token to the user. Then, the user sends the token to the application or service; the service will validate the token against the STS again before giving the user access to the system.

To collaborate with other organizations, you can establish trust relationships with other organizations that have implemented claims-based authentication. You can establish these trust relationships at the IdP level. By setting up these relationships, partner organizations can sign in using their credentials, retrieve an authorization token from the STS, and then sign into different applications.

The following diagram shows a high-level overview of the flow that's used in claims-based authentication:

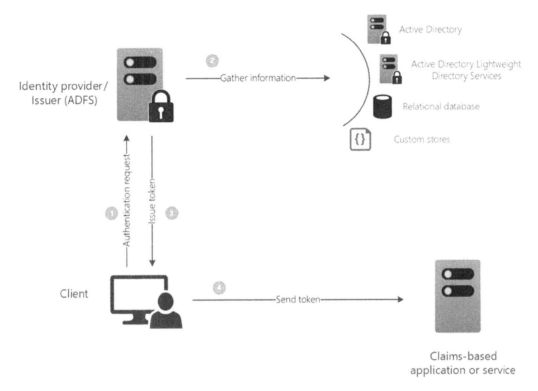

Figure 4.1 – Claims-based authentication

Let's look at these steps in detail:

1. The client makes an authentication request.

2. The request is redirected to the STS. The STS interacts with the user to gather and validate the necessary credentials (username/password, MFA, passwordless, and so on). The STS will gather information in an identity store that supports claims-based authentication.

3. The STS will package the attributes of the user coming from the identity store into claims and put that into a secure and signed token that will be sent back to the client.

4. The client receives the token from the IDP, which now identifies the user to the application.

Next, we'll have a look at the advantages of this approach.

Benefits of claims-based identity

Claims-based identity has several benefits over the traditional username and password authentication process. With claims-based identity, you decouple the authentication mechanism from applications and services. This is all handled by an external and dedicated issuer or IdP. You can also replace roles with claims in your applications, which will give you a more flexible and granular set of attributes that can be used for authorization. Then, these roles can be added to the claims. Besides that, it can reduce the burden of provisioning and maintaining the identities in your organization. This is all handled for you by the external IdP. Finally, you can set up trust relationships with other organizations and partners that use claims-based authentication. This will provide access to the applications and services in your organization and vice versa.

Claims-based authentication can be found in many applications, such as Azure Active Directory Federation Services, Microsoft SharePoint 2010 and 2013, applications that use Windows Identity Foundation, and Windows access control services. It is also heavily used for applications running on-premises and in the cloud.

Now that we have covered the basics of claims-based identity, let's look at first-generation protocols.

First-generation protocols

The first claims-based protocols appeared in the early 2000s. Two of these protocols are still supported and heavily used by Azure Active Directory and Windows Server Active Directory. These two protocols are SAML and WS-Federation. Both are used to provide cross-domain **Single Sign-On (SSO)**, which is a scenario that the authentication protocols that were popular at that time didn't handle very well, such as username and password authentication. To handle these scenarios, cookies, a very popular and widely used mechanism, were used.

In the next section, we are going to look at SSO in more detail.

Single sign-on

With SSO, users can sign into several related but independent systems or applications by using a single username and password. True SSO allows the user to sign in only once and then access services without re-entering their authentication credentials, such as their username and password. The simplest form of SSO can be achieved over IP networks using cookies, but this is only possible if the website shares a common DNS parent domain.

In the next section, we are going to look at cookies.

Cookies

Users interact with web applications in a very straightforward way. The user makes a request to a website using a URL in the browser; the web server receives the request, runs some business logic as a response to that request, and then the server proceeds by returning HTML to the user with the required information in it. The user will then interact with the returned HTML web page by pressing a button, for instance, and then the whole process will repeat itself. From an authentication perspective, every round trip that is made to the web server needs to know which user is considered the current requestor. The pre-claims way of handling this can be broken down into three steps:

1. The application will ask the user to identify themselves by asking them to provide a username and password.

2. Once the user has specified their credentials, they will be sent over to the web server and validated by the application. When these credentials have been validated, the application will create a **session cookie**, which represents the successful outcome of the authentication process for the domain where the application is hosted. This cookie will also hold some information about the user, including a reference to the session data, and will be signed and encrypted so that only the application can read and modify it.

3. Every additional request that's made to the application will carry the session cookie with it. The application will retrieve the cookie from each request and verify it. This session cookie will also replace the need to authenticate by providing a username and password. The current user scope will be part of that session cookie for the duration of the session. Cookies will typically have a limited validity duration to minimize abuse.

These session cookies are stored by web browsers. These web browsers will also send these cookies with every request that's made to the application automatically, without the need for developers to write any additional code for this. The life cycle of the cookies is handled by the browser automatically.

This mechanism is not very supportive for scenarios where you want to implement SSO and each application implements authentication independently. Because the session cookie is stored for a particular domain, it cannot be reused by applications that are hosted on different domains. The session cookie is not valid there. This means that you simply cannot set up SSO across different domains using this mechanism.

In the next section, we are going to look at SAML in more depth and how this can help you implement SSO.

SAML

We introduced SAML briefly earlier in this chapter, but we are going to cover it here in more depth. SAML originated in the early 2000s to solve the problem that arose with SSO with cookies. Individuals from more than 24 companies collaborated to create a solution to this SSO problem. SAML 2.0, which is based on XML, is the most adopted version of SAML and is still used in a lot of solutions.

SAML solves the SSO problem by adding another abstraction layer. Instead of relying on the browser's functionality for handling cookies, it introduces a sequence of messages at the application level. This allows the application to send authentication requests and obtain tokens that can be sent across different domains. These tokens can then be validated by the target and used to initialize a new session within the new domain. This is in line with the inner workings of claims-based authentication, although the terminology that SAML uses is sometimes a bit different.

SAML introduced two different technologies: the protocol and the token format. The tokens are called **assertions** and they contain a package of security information, and they are signed with a cryptographic key. They are used by IdPs to pack the different user attributes and transfer them across different domains and applications.

The following is an example of a SAML request message:

```
<samlp:AuthnRequest
xmlns:samlp="urn:oasis:names:tc:SAML:2.0:protocol"
xmlns:saml="urn:oasis:names:tc:SAML:2.0:assertion"
ID="ONELOGIN_809707f0030a5d00620c9d9df97f627afe9dcc24"
Version="2.0" ProviderName="SP test" IssueInstant="2014-07-
16T23:52:45Z" Destination="http://idp.example.com/SSOService.
php" ProtocolBinding="urn:oasis:names:tc:SAML:2.0:bindings:HT
TP-POST" AssertionConsumerServiceURL="http://sp.example.com/
demo1/index.php?acs">
  <saml:Issuer>http://sp.example.com/demo1/metadata.php</
saml:Issuer>
  <samlp:NameIDPolicy Format="urn:oasis:names:tc:SAML:1.1:name
id-format:emailAddress" AllowCreate="true"/>
  <samlp:RequestedAuthnContext Comparison="exact">
    <saml:AuthnContextClassRef>urn:oasis:names:tc:SAML:2.0:
ac:classes:PasswordProtectedTransport</
saml:AuthnContextClassRef>
  </samlp:RequestedAuthnContext>
</samlp:AuthnRequest>
```

The fact that SAML assertions are based on XML makes them very powerful, flexible, and easy for developers to read and write. However, XML is very verbose, which leads to big tokens. Another drawback is that pieces of code in XML can be expressed in multiple ways. This can lead to problems when signatures need to be created and validated. A different representation of the SAML document can lead to breaking a signature's verification.

SAML defines a lot of messages that support various sign-in and sign-out flows. For instance, you can create a single message that signs a user out of all applications that are part of the SSO session.

SAML provides a lot of interesting mechanisms for supporting SSO across different domains. This gives the impression that it can also be used in modern application development. However, because tokens are quite big and the same document can be expressed in multiple ways, this makes it less suitable for modern application development. However, the majority of SaaS solutions today, especially the big ones, still use SAML.

In the next section, we are going to look into WS-Federation.

WS-Federation

WS-Federation is a protocol that's used by non-browser applications. In the early 2000s, non-browser applications also suffered from cross-domain integration problems. For these types of applications, the scenario of being separated by organizational and network boundaries also became valid. To solve this issue, several companies worked together to create a set of protocols to overcome these challenges. They created a set of protocols, languages, and frameworks that defined how to ensure secure, reliable, and interoperable communication between different software components, regardless of their location or hosting platform. This collaboration led to a long list of specifications, collectively known as **web-service** (**WS***). For each aspect of communication between applications and services, a different specification was provided with the idea that, during implementation, only the features that were needed could be used.

WS* was used heavily in .NET 3.0, **Windows Communication Foundation** (**WCF**), and **Active Directory Federation Services** (**ADFS**). Applications that are still based on WCF, for instance, are still using it. However, most modern applications don't use it anymore because it's complex and applications are more REST-based now. WS-Federation was one of these specifications, and it focused on how users from one given organization could access resources that were managed by other organizations. WS-Federation also covered these features for browser-based applications, which are still used in applications nowadays. It addresses a lot of scenarios that SAML addresses. However, the main difference is that the messages are a lot simpler, and they are based on HTTP requests. You can use it directly for SOAP-based applications and web applications.

The following is an example of an ADFS 2.0 WS-Federation request:

```
GET https://packt.pub.net/adfs/ls/?wa=wsignin1.0&wtrealm=app1.
rcbj.net&wctx=edcd55c4-ac15-483c-9f19-f19933f6a79d&wct=2021-10-
06T21%3a59%3a01Z
```

Now that we have covered some of the first-generation protocols, let's look at modern protocols.

Modern protocols

The protocols that we described previously were mostly used in an era where internet usage was not as high as it is nowadays. These days, in a lot of countries, almost everyone has a smartphone, tablet, and/or computer and uses the internet. As we are spending more and more time online, and we are using more and more different websites and applications, the need arose to combine different services into a single workflow.

For instance, let's say you are a big social media user and you have several social media accounts. You only want to publish your messages once across these different social media channels. For this to work, an application should be able to sign in to these different accounts and post content on your behalf.

This was originally implemented by the most infamous antipattern in history, known as the **password-sharing antipattern**, as shown in the following diagram:

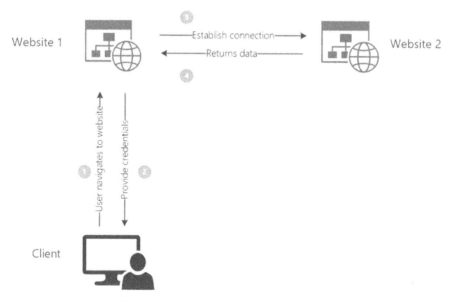

Fig 4.2 – The password-sharing antipattern

Let's look at these steps in detail:

1. The user navigates to **Website 1**. This website needs access to the user's resources from **Website 2**.

2. **Website 1** prompts the user to provide the credentials for **Website 2**.

3. **Website 1** uses these credentials to sign into **Website 2** and accesses the data and resources from that website on behalf of the user.

4. **Website 2** is not aware of the fact that **Website 1** is in the middle of it and thinks that it is been dealing with the user directly. **Website 2** returns the data to **Website 1**.

However, this is not a secure solution. **Website 1** is handling authentication for you, has access to the credentials, and can perform all sorts of activity on **Website 2**. These credentials can also be stored somewhere, logged, and more. This risk can become much bigger if you are reusing passwords for multiple websites and services.

This was a big issue that needed to be solved. The solution came with the birth of OAuth2, which we will cover in the next section.

OAuth

The need to grant access to other resources led to the creation of OAuth, an authorization framework that allows you to approve the process of an application interacting with another on your behalf without you giving away your password. It started with OAuth 1.0, which was co-created by people from Twitter, Google, Yahoo!, and Ma.gnolia around 2006.

OAuth 1.0 was capable of solving the delegation access scenario between web applications. However, it had a lot of shortcomings, some of which are as follows:

*   It did not support revocation very well.

*   The architecture was not suitable for scenarios other than web app-to-web app server communication.

*   Clients needed to adhere to strong cryptographic requirements.

This was the reason OAuth2 was created, which solved these issues and supported other application scenarios.

OAuth 2.0 is now an industry standard and used in all sorts of applications and supported by all identity and access management solutions and cloud providers.

In the next chapter, *Chapter 5, Securing Applications with OAuth 2.0, OpenID Connect, and MSAL*, we will cover OAuth 2.0 in more depth, including the different flows that are supported.

Summary

In this chapter, we learned how identity protocols have evolved to answer the different needs in application development and to secure different systems. First, we covered two very basic elements – authentication and authorization. Then, we covered the different authentication techniques and protocols, such as password-based authentication, claims-based authentication, and more. We finished this chapter by providing a brief introduction to OAuth 2.0. This chapter gave you an overview of how authentication protocols have evolved and specified what the main drivers were, from an application perspective, for helping create the modern authentication protocols that we use nowadays.

In the next chapter, we are going to build on this and cover OAuth 2.0 in depth. We are also going to look at OpenID Connect and MSAL in more detail and learn how these protocols and techniques can help developers build robust and secure applications that can be hosted everywhere.

Further reading

Check out the following links for more information about the topics that were covered in this chapter:

- *Authentication versus authorization*: `https://auth0.com/docs/get-started/authentication-and-authorization`

- *Password-based authentication with Azure Active Directory*: `https://docs.microsoft.com/en-us/azure/active-directory/fundamentals/auth-password-based-sso`

- *Integrated Windows Authentication*: `https://docs.microsoft.com/en-us/aspnet/web-api/overview/security/integrated-windows-authentication`

- *A Guide to Claims-Based Identity and Access Control, Second Edition*, by Dominick Baier, Vittorio Bertocci, Keith Brown, Matias Woloski, Eugenio Pace – book download: `https://www.microsoft.com/en-us/download/details.aspx?id=28362`

- *How SAML Authentication Works*: `https://auth0.com/blog/how-saml-authentication-works/`

- *Web Services Federation protocol*: `https://auth0.com/docs/protocols/ws-fed-protocol`

- *OAuth 2.0*: `https://oauth.net/2/`

5
Securing Applications with OAuth 2.0, OpenID Connect, and MSAL

In the previous chapter, we covered the basics of authentication and how this has evolved into modern authentication protocols. We covered password-based authentication, claims-based authentication, and more.

In this chapter, we are going to take a deep dive into these modern authentication protocols. We are going to cover OAuth 2.0, OpenID Connect, and the **Microsoft Authentication Library** (**MSAL**) in greater depth. Finally, we will finish this chapter by building a secure and modern application using these techniques, protocols, and frameworks.

In this chapter, the following topics will be covered:

- The OAuth 2.0 framework and its specifications
- OAuth 2.0 flows
- The OpenID Connect protocol and its specifications
- An overview of the Microsoft Identity Web authentication library
- An overview of MSAL
- Securing your application using OAuth 2.0, OpenID Connect, and MSAL

Let's get started!

Technical requirements

To follow along with this chapter, you will need to have an active Azure Active Directory tenant. The Azure Active Directory tenant was created in *Chapter 1*, *Microsoft Identity Platform Overview*. Also, you will need to have the latest version of Visual Studio or Visual Studio Code installed:

- Visual Studio Code: `https://code.visualstudio.com/`
- Visual Studio: `https://visualstudio.microsoft.com/`

For the examples in this chapter, I'm going to use Visual Studio Code, but of course, you can use Visual Studio.

You can download the source code for this chapter at `https://github.com/PacktPublishing/Azure-Active-Directory-for-Developers/tree/main/Chapter%205`.

The OAuth 2.0 framework and its specifications

In the previous chapter, we briefly covered OAuth and why this protocol is well suited for modern applications. OAuth is an authorization framework that is specifically designed to meet the security scenarios that are required nowadays for authenticating users and connecting various services together.

The OAuth 2.0 authorization framework is a delegation protocol that provides the user with the ability to grant an application or service access to protected resources without impersonating the user and revealing their credentials. To do this, OAuth 2.0 introduces an authorization layer where the role of the client is separated from the role of the resource owner. The application can request authorization from the owner of the resource, and it will receive tokens that it can use to access those resources. This token represents delegated permissions to access the resource, without the need for the application to impersonate the user who controls the resource. By using a valid OAuth token, access to the resources can be granted and limited to only the actions that the resource owner has delegated.

The most common format that is used for access tokens is the **JSON Web Token (JWT)** format. Officially, it is not part of the OAuth 2.0 specifications, but most identity providers use this format. JWT tokens offer a very effective and secure way of transmitting information between different parties. The permissions that are passed into the access token are called **scopes**. When a client or application uses OAuth for authentication, it specifies the scopes that are needed to access resources. When these scopes are also authorized by the user, the access token will include these authorized scopes.

Let's make this clearer by using an example. In this scenario, we have a custom-built document storage service in Azure and a custom-built cloud printing service that is also hosted in Azure. The documents need to be printed by the printing service. Both services can communicate with each other using an API. Here, the only constraint is that both services are owned by different companies, so they are stored in separate Azure AD tenants. In this scenario, you cannot set up a direct connection between the two services. By using OAuth, you can delegate access to the documents across these two services, without providing your password to the printing service.

To summarize, OAuth is all about getting the right of access from one service to another service. The client application wants to get access, on behalf of a resource owner, to a protected resource. Usually, the resource owner is the end user of the system. Additionally, OAuth defines several roles, which we will look at next.

Roles

In most OAuth 2.0 flows, there are four different roles or parties involved in the exchange:

- **Resource owner**: This is the entity that grants access to a protected resource. In most scenarios, the resource owner is the end user. However, this could also be another resource that could act on its own behalf. The data is owned by the resource owner, and it has the permissions to allow clients to access the data or the resource.

- **Resource server**: This is the location where the data resides or the server that is hosting the protected resource. It is capable of accepting and responding to protected resources using a bearer access token.

- **Client**: This refers to an application or service that is making a protected resource request on behalf of the resource owner and using the authorization that the resource owner has. Clients can be applications, users, servers, desktops, and other devices.

- **Authorization server**: Access tokens are issued by the authorization server to the client after the successful authentication of the resource owner and after receiving the authorization that belongs to the resource owner. The authorization servers are also referred to as identity providers. They are responsible for securely handling anything that has to do with the user's access and information, along with the trust relationship between the flow.

In the following diagram, you can see the different roles in the exchange process, with the Microsoft identity platform positioned inside it:

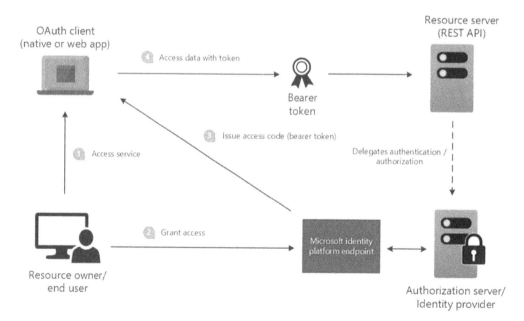

Figure 5.1 – The OAuth parties

In the preceding diagram, you can see that the Microsoft identity platform endpoint is positioned in front of the authorization server. Every application (or OAuth client) that wants to accept either personal Microsoft accounts or Azure AD enterprise accounts (or both) to sign users in must be registered in Azure AD using the Azure portal's app registration experience, PowerShell, the CLI, or the Microsoft Graph API. Once you have registered the app, it communicates with the Microsoft identity platform endpoint by sending requests to it, using Open ID Connect and OAuth 2.0 for transport. The endpoints that it communicates with are the following:

```
https://login.microsoftonline.com/{tenant}/oauth2/v2.0/
authorize
https://login.microsoftonline.com/{tenant}/oauth2/v2.0/token
```

The {tenant} value can consist of the following four values:

- **Organizations**: Replacing {tenant} with organizations will result in only users with work/school accounts from Azure AD being allowed to sign in to the application.

- **Consumers**: Replacing {tenant} with consumers will result in only users with personal Microsoft accounts being allowed to sign in to the application.

- **Common**: Replacing {tenant} with common will allow users with both work/school accounts from any Azure AD tenant and personal Microsoft accounts to sign in to the application.

- **Specific tenant**: Replacing {tenant} with either the tenant's ID (such as 4aeff021-7g34-6kf7-2bcc-6jh2k6b6a230) or the friendly domain name of the Azure tenant (packt.onmicrosoft.com) allows users with accounts associated with the tenant where the app is registered to sign in to the application. Additionally, the endpoints support Azure AD B2B users, who can authenticate with a personal account in the tenant.

In the next section, we are going to cover the abstract flow in OAuth 2.0, where you will see how the different parties generally interact with each other in the exchange.

The OAuth 2.0 abstract flow

The OAuth 2.0 abstract flow, as illustrated in the following diagram, describes the interactions between the four parties:

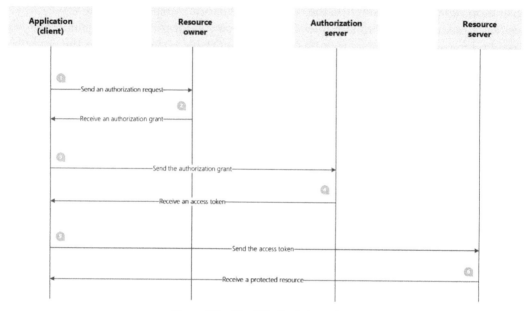

Figure 5.2 – The OAuth abstract flow

The preceding abstract flow involves the following steps:

1. An authorization request is made by the client to the resource owner.

2. The authorization grant is received by the client in the form of a credential. This credential is a representation of the authorization of the resource owner.

3. An access token is requested by the client. This token can be used to access the protected resources.

4. The client is authenticated by the authorization server. The server validates the authorization grant. When the authorization grant becomes valid, the access token is issued and returned to the client.

5. The client sends a new request to the protected resource and uses the access token for authorization.

6. The access token is then validated by the resource server. If valid, the request is served, and the requested data is sent back inside the response.

We have now covered the abstract flow. The actual flow used in authentication scenarios depends on the authorization grant type that is used and supported by the authorization server. The OAuth framework supports several grant types for different use cases. These types will be covered later in this chapter. In the next section, we will take a look at tokens.

Tokens

Tokens are at the base of all OAuth transactions. OAuth (along with OpenID Connect, which will be covered later) makes extensive use of **access tokens** or **bearer tokens**. These bearer tokens are security tokens that are used to grant the *bearer* access to the protected resources that reside on the resource server. This means that anyone who has a copy of this bearer token can have access to the data. The access tokens are the key mechanism that is at the center of the entire ecosystem of OAuth. Without these tokens, there is simply no OAuth.

Clients fetch tokens from the authorization server, such as the Microsoft identity platform, to pass on to the protected resource. The tokens are created by the authorization server; they identify the resource owner (user) and include client permissions (scopes).

There is one important item to note here: unlike some other security tokens, bearer tokens do not have built-in features to prevent unauthorized parties from using them. This means that the exchange of this token between the client and the authorization server should be secured. If these steps are not taken, it is possible that the token can be intercepted and used by an unintended party. This means that they should be transported using the HTTPS protocol. These principles also apply when it comes to storing and caching these tokens.

There are three types of tokens used in OAuth 2.0 (and OpenID Connect):

- **ID tokens**: These types of tokens are received by the client from the authorization server. These tokens are used to sign a user in and also get the basic profile information about that user.
- **Access tokens**: These types of tokens are received by a resource server from the client, which holds the permissions that the client is granted access to.
- **Refresh tokens**: When an application is authorized, it is issued a refresh token that can be used to get new access tokens for the resources without user interaction.

In the next section, we will cover OpenID Connect in more detail.

The OpenID Connect protocol and its specifications

Azure AD uses the OpenID Connect protocol to power the sign-in flows. OpenID Connect is an authentication protocol that is built on top of OAuth 2.0. This identity layer can be used to securely sign in a user to an application. When using the implementation provided by the Microsoft identity platform, you can also make use of features to sign users in and add API access to your apps.

OAuth 2.0 provides an **authorization** protocol, and OpenID Connect extends this protocol to be used as an **authentication** protocol. You can perform single sign-on using OAuth by extending this to an authentication protocol with OpenID Connect. To enable clients to verify the identity of the user, OpenID Connect introduces a security token that is called the **ID token**. OpenID Connect specifies that ID tokens are JWTs. There is basic profile information about the user stored in this ID token. Additionally, OpenID Connect introduces an **UserInfo Endpoint**, which is an API that can return information about the user.

In the following diagram, you can see an overview of the OpenID Connect specifications that are important for the flow of signing in a user using Azure AD and OAuth 2.0:

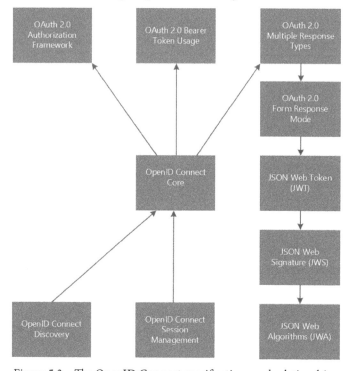

Figure 5.3 – The OpenID Connect specifications and relationships

Here, we will briefly cover the different items:

- **OpenID Connect Core**: The OpenID Connect Core specification describes the format of the authentication requests and response messages for the hybrid flow, the authorization code flow, and the implicit flow. Additionally, it describes the format of `id_token` in detail and covers the different claim types that are part of `id_token` for storing basic profile information about the user. It also describes the UserInfo endpoint API in detail (for more information, you can refer to `https://openid.net/specs/openid-connect-core-1_0.html`).

- **OpenID Connect Discovery**: OpenID Connect provides a mechanism in terms of how clients can dynamically discover information about OpenID providers. It obtains the information that is needed to interact with the identity provider/authorization server (for more information, you can refer to `https://openid.net/specs/openid-connect-discovery-1_0.html`).

- **OAuth 2.0 Multiple Response Types**: These specifications provide guidance on how to control which tokens need to be returned in a response to an authentication request, along with the HTTP mechanism that should be used. To do this, it defines a `response_type` request parameter for the returned tokens and `response_mode` for the mechanism (for more information, you can refer to `https://openid.net/specs/oauth-v2-multiple-response-types-1_0.html`).

- **OpenID Connection Session Management**: This specification describes how to manage sessions, including when to log out a user/client (for more information, you can refer to `https://openid.net/specs/openid-connect-session-1_0.html`).

- **JSON Web Token (JWT)**: Clients will receive the user's identity encoded in a secure JWT, which is called the ID token in OpenID Connect. JWTs can support a wide range of signature and encryption algorithms such as **JSON Web Signature (JWS)** and **JSON Web Algorithms (JWA)**. For more information, you can refer to `https://datatracker.ietf.org/doc/html/rfc7519`.

- **JSON Web Signatures (JWS)**: This provides content that has been secured with digital signatures (for more information, you can refer to `https://datatracker.ietf.org/doc/html/rfc7515`.

- **JSON Web Algorithms (JWA)**: This provides cryptographic algorithms and identifiers to be used with the JWS. For more information, please refer to `https://datatracker.ietf.org/doc/html/rfc7518`.

Nowadays, OpenID Connect is the leading industry best practice for identity provisioning and single sign-on. It uses a successful formula: simple JSON-based identity tokens (JWTs) that are all delivered via OAuth 2.0 flows, which have been fully designed for a wide range of application types.

In the next section, we will examine the different OAuth 2.0 and OpenID Connect flows.

The OAuth 2.0 and OpenID Connect flows

Now that we have covered OAuth 2.0 and OpenID Connect, we can move on to the flows that both of them support. Both OAuth and OpenID Connect provide different flows for different scenarios and application types.

In the upcoming sections, we are going to cover these different types of grant flows, starting with the authorization code flow. Additionally, we are going to cover how the Microsoft identity platform handles these flows.

OpenID Connect using the implicit flow

With OpenID Connect, you can securely sign users into an application. By using the Microsoft identity platform's implementation of OpenID Connect, sign-in and API access are added to your applications.

As mentioned earlier, OpenID Connect extends the OAuth 2.0 authorization protocol so that it can be used as an authentication protocol. In this way, you can implement single sign-on using OAuth. OpenID Connect includes an ID token for this purpose, which is a security token that the client uses to verify the identity of the user. Additionally, this token retrieves basic profile information about this user, and it introduces the UserInfo endpoint, which is an API that returns information about the signed-in user.

One way to implement OpenID Connect is to use the implicit flow. Nowadays, this is only appropriate for web apps that use the authorization code flow (see the following diagram) for `access_tokens` and the implicit flow for ID tokens. This combination of authorization code and implicit is referred to as a **hybrid flow**.

In the following diagram, you can see the protocol diagram for the implicit flow:

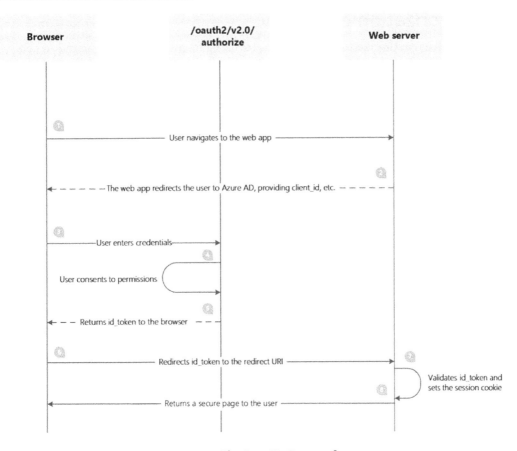

Figure 5.4 – The OpenID Connect flow

The implicit flow involves the following steps:

1.   The user navigates to the web app.

2.   The web app redirects the user to Azure AD, providing the app's `client_id`.

3.   The user enters the credentials to sign in.

4.   The user consents to the permissions that will be given to the app.

5.   The `id_token` is returned to the browser by the web server.

6.   The `id_token` is sent to the redirect URI of the server.

7.   The `id_token` is validated, and the session cookie is set.

8.   Finally, the secured page is returned to the user.

In the next section, we are going to cover the authorization code flow.

The authorization code flow

The first OAuth 2.0 authorization flow that we are going to cover is the authorization code flow. Typically, this flow is used in scenarios where apps, which have been installed onto a device, want to get access to protected resources, such as web APIs.

This flow is used for the majority of apps and application types, which includes web apps, single-page apps, and natively installed apps such as mobile or desktop apps. Apps can securely obtain access tokens using this flow. These tokens can then be used to access protected resources that have been secured by the Microsoft identity platform. It also provides refresh tokens to get additional access tokens when the access tokens expire.

Here, you can see the protocol diagram for the authorization code flow:

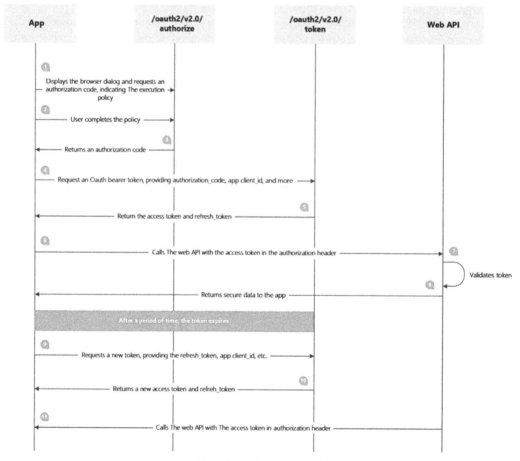

Figure 5.5 – The authorization code flow

The authorization code flow involves the following steps:

1. The app displays a browser dialog, a request, and an authorization code, which indicates the execution policy.

2. The user completes the policy.

3. An authorization code is returned to the app.

4. The app requests an OAuth bearer token, providing the `authorization_code`, the app's `client_id`, and more, from the token endpoint.

5. The token endpoint returns an access token and a refresh token.

6. The application uses this access token in the authorization header to call the web API.

7. The token is validated by the web API.

8. Once validated, the secure data is returned to the app.

9. After a while, the access token will become invalid. The app will request a new token, providing the refresh token, app client, and more.

10. The token endpoint will return a new access token and a refresh token.

11. The application uses this access token again in the authorization header to call the web API, and the secure data will be returned once more.

In the next section, we are going to cover the **On-Behalf-Of (OBO)** flow.

The OBO flow

The OBO flow is used in scenarios where an app invokes a web API or service, which, in turn, needs to call another web API or service on behalf of the user. In this scenario, the user identity is passed on through the request chain. The middle-tier service needs a secure access token from the Microsoft identity platform to make an authenticated request to the downstream API or service.

Note that this flow only works for user principals. A service principal can't request an app-only token, send it to the API, and then have the API exchange that token for another token that represents the original service principal. Another important aspect to bear in mind is that the OBO flow is acting on another party's behalf, which is also called the **delegated scenario**. This means that, in terms of permissions, it is only using **delegated scopes** and not **application roles**.

In *Figure 5.6*, you can see the protocol diagram for the OBO flow:

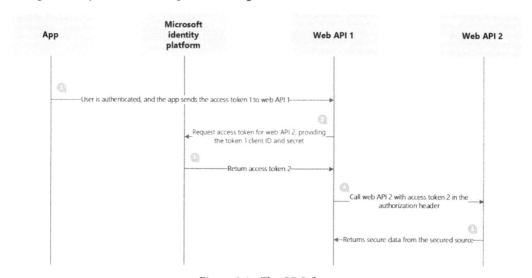

Figure 5.6 – The OBO flow

The OBO flow involves the following steps:

1. The user is authenticated, and the app sends access token 1 to **Web API 1**.

2. **Web API 1** will request an access token from **Microsoft Identity platform** for **Web API 2**, providing the token 1 client ID and the client secret.

3. Then, **Microsoft Identity platform** will return access token 2 to **Web API 1**.

4. **Web API 1** will call **Web API 2** with access token 2 in the authorization header.

5. **Web API 2** will return secure data from the secured source.

In the next section, we will cover the client credentials flow.

The client credentials flow

The client credentials flow, which is also called two-legged OAuth, uses the identity of the app to access web-hosted resources. This type of grant is used for server-to-server interactions that don't need immediate interaction with the user in scenarios where operations run in the background. These types of applications are referred to as *service accounts* or *daemon apps*.

With the client credentials flow, instead of acting on behalf of a user, applications use their own credentials to authenticate to another web service or API. In these scenarios, the Microsoft identity platform also provides the ability to use certificates as a credential (instead of a shared secret). Because the flow uses the application's own credentials, these credentials should be kept safe. Never store the credentials in your source code or configuration files; instead, use secure storage such as Azure Key Vault.

In this flow, the administrator grants the permissions directly to the application. Since there is no user involved in the authentication process, the resource will enforce that the application has the authorization to perform an action.

Here, you can see the protocol diagram for the client credentials flow:

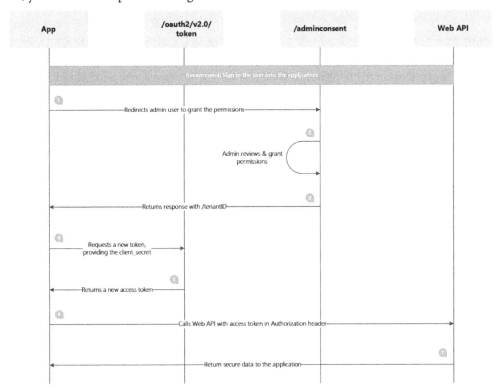

Figure 5.7 – The client credentials flow

The client credentials flow involves the following steps:

1. The app redirects the admin user to grant the permissions.
2. The `adminconsent` endpoint will review the admin permissions and grant the permissions.
3. The `adminconsent` endpoint returns a response that includes `/tenantID`.
4. The app requests a new token, providing the `client_secret`.
5. The token endpoint will return a new access token.
6. The app will call the web API with the access token included inside the authorization header.
7. The web API will return the secure data to the application.

In the next section, we are going to cover the **Resource Owner Password Credentials (ROPC)** flow.

The ROPC flow

The ROPC flow allows applications to directly sign users in using a password.

Microsoft does not recommend using this flow for your applications. There are a lot of alternative flows that offer a higher grade of security and don't require a high degree of trust in the application. In addition to this, this flow will also expose a lot of risk to your application and will conflict with several features that are provided alongside the Microsoft identity platform.

The Microsoft identity platform only allows support for the ROPC flow for Azure AD tenants, not personal accounts. Personal accounts that are invited to an Azure AD tenant, for instance, by using Azure AD B2B, cannot use the ROPC flow either. Accounts that don't have a password and that use features such as the Microsoft authenticator app, FIDO, or SMS sign-in are also not able to use this flow. Additionally, the ROPC flow is not supported in most hybrid scenarios.

This flow should only be used in scenarios where more secure flows are not an option.

The following diagram shows the protocol diagram for the ROPC flow:

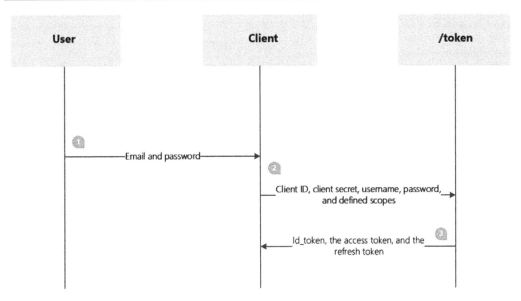

Figure 5.8 – The ROPC flow

The ROPC flow involves the following steps:

1. The user will provide an email address and a password to the client.

2. The client will send the client ID, client secret, username, and password, including the scopes that are defined, to the /token endpoint.

3. The /token endpoint will return the id_token, the access token, and the refresh token to the client.

In the next section, we will cover the device code flow.

The device code flow

The device code flow is also a supported flow within the Microsoft identity platform. This flow allows users to sign in to devices that are input-constrained, such as printers, IoT devices, smart TVs, and more. This flow is enabled when a user visits a web page on their device browser to sign in. Once the user is signed in, the device can retrieve access tokens and refresh tokens when needed.

Here, you can see a protocol diagram for the device code flow:

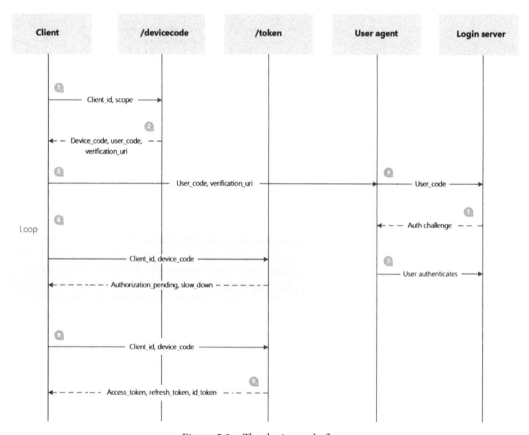

Figure 5.9 – The device code flow

The device code flow involves the following steps:

1. The client will provide the app's `client_id` and scope to the `/devicecode` endpoint.

2. The `/devicecode` endpoint will return `device_code`, `user_code`, and the verification URI to the client.

3. The client will then send the `user_code` and the `verification_URI` to the user agent.

4. Following this, the user agent will send the `user_code` to the login server.

5. The login server will return an auth challenge to the user agent. The user has 15 minutes to sign in.

6. The client will wait for the authorization of the user.

7. The user will then authenticate to the login server.

8. Once the user has been authenticated, both `client_id` and `device_code` are sent to the `/token` endpoint.

9. The `/token` endpoint will return the access token, the refresh token, and the ID token to the client.

> **Important Note**
>
> In the future, third-party cookies will be removed from browsers. When that happens, the implicit grant flow will no longer be a suitable authentication method. Without the third-party cookies to rely on, the silent SSO features of the implicit flow will no longer work. For these scenarios, the authorization code flow with PKCE is now the recommended authentication method.

Now that we have a better understanding of the specifications of OpenID Connect, in the next section, we are going to cover OpenID Connect middleware.

An overview of the Microsoft Identity Web authentication library

The Microsoft Identity Web library offers support for ASP.NET Core applications to integrate with the Microsoft identity platform. These libraries simplify adding authentication and authorization support to web APIs and web applications. These libraries provide a layer that forms the glue between ASP.NET Core, the ASP.NET Core authentication layer, and MSAL for .NET.

The Microsoft Identity Web authentication library is available as a set of packages on NuGet. These packages can be easily installed using the NuGet Package Manager in Visual Studio or the `dotnet add` .NET CLI command in Visual Studio Code. They are included in .NET 5.0 and can also be downloaded for ASP.NET Core 3.1 projects.

Microsoft Identity Web provides the following four packages:

- `Microsoft.Identity.Web`: This is the primary and mandatory library for all apps that use Microsoft Identity Web for authentication and authorization.
- `Microsoft.Identity.Web.UI`: This is an optional library. By using this package, a UI will be added for user sign-in and sign-out functionality and it will also add an associate controller for web apps.
- `Microsoft.Identity.Web.MicrosoftGraph`: This is also an optional library that adds support for simplified interactions with the Microsoft Graph API.
- `Microsoft.Identity.Web.MicrosoftGraphBeta`: This is also optional and adds support for interaction with the Microsoft Graph API beta endpoint.

You can easily enable these packages when you create a new .NET Core application. By specifying this during the creation of a new project, the necessary packages are added during creation. An example of this can be seen in the following command used to create a new .NET Core web app. This command will add the Microsoft Identity Web libraries to the project, including the starter code:

```
dotnet new webapi --auth SingleOrg
```

In the following table, you can see which app types are supported, including regular arguments. This data is taken from the official Microsoft documentation website:

Scenario	Command	Template		Audience	Call web API (optional)
The MVC API		webapi		SingleOrg	
The MVC web app		Mvc			--calls-graph**
The Razor web app		webapp		MultiOrg*	
Blazor Server	dotnet new	blazorserver	--auth		--called-api-scopes "scopes" --called-api-url webAPIUrl
Blazor WebAssembly		Blazorwasm Blazorwasm --hosted		IndivdualB2C	

Table 5.1 – Supported types

* By default, `MultiOrg` is not supported with `webapi`, but it can be enabled in `appsettings.json` by setting the tenant to either `common` or `organizations`.

** `--calls-graph` is not supported for Azure AD B2C.

As you can see in the preceding table, the following authentication options are available for Azure AD and Azure AD B2C:

- `SingleOrg`: Organizational authentication for a single tenant

- `MultiOrg`: Organizational authentication for multiple tenants

- `IndividualB2C`: Individual authentication with Azure AD B2C

ASP.NET Core Identity also provides functionality for authentication and authorization; however, there are features in the Microsoft Identity Web packages that aren't available in the ASP.NET Core identity. In the following table, you will get an overview of the differences between the packages (the following table is taken from the official Microsoft documentation website):

Feature	ASP.NET Core 3.1	Microsoft Identity Web
Web app user sign-in	Work or school accounts Azure AD B2C social identities	Work or school accounts Personal Microsoft accounts Azure AD B2C social identities
Web API protection	Work or school accounts Azure AD B2C social identities	Work or school accounts Personal Microsoft accounts Azure AD B2C social identities
Multi-tenant apps issuer validation	NA	Azure AD B2C and all clouds
Web app/API calls Microsoft Graph	NA	Yes
Web app/API calls web API	NA	Yes
Certificate credentials support	NA	Yes, including Azure Key Vault
Support for conditional access and incremental consent in web apps	NA	Yes, in Blazor, Razor pages, and MVC
Web API token encryption certificates	NA	Yes
Web API scopes/app role validation	NA	Yes
Web API WWW-Authenticate header generation	NA	Yes

Table 5.2 – The differences between the packages

When building cloud applications, the Microsoft Identity Web packages are the preferred packages for authentication and authorization, as you can see in the preceding overview.

Now that we have a better understanding of the Microsoft Identity Web authentication library and how to create ASP.NET Core applications easily with the integration of the library, in the next section, we will cover MSAL.

An overview of MSAL

MSAL is specifically created to acquire tokens from the Microsoft identity platform. These tokens are used to authenticate the users and access secured resources. You can use MSAL libraries for a variety of languages. It has support for .NET, Python, JavaScript, Java, Android, Go (Preview), and iOS, and it can be used to provide secure access to web APIs, third-party web APIs, the Microsoft Graph API, and other Microsoft APIs.

There is support for the following platforms and frameworks:

- **MSAL for Android**: This supports the Android platform.

- **MSAL Angular**: This supports the Angular and Angular.js frameworks in single-page apps.

- **MSAL for iOS and macOS**: This supports both iOS and macOS.

- **MSAL Go (Preview)**: This supports Windows, macOS, and Linux.

- **MSAL Java**: This supports Windows, macOS, and Linux.

- **MSAL.js**: This supports the JavaScript/TypeScript frameworks, such as Durandal.js, Ember.js, and Vue.js.

- **MSAL.NET**: This supports .NET Core, .NET Framework, Xamarin iOS, Xamarin Android, and Universal Windows Platform.

- **MSAL Node**: This supports desktop apps with Electron, cross-platform console apps, and web apps with Express.

- **MSAL Python**: This supports Windows, macOS, and Linux.

- **MSAL React**: This supports the React and React-based libraries (such as Next.js and Gatsby.js) in single-page apps.

> **Important Note**
> Languages and frameworks will be added and possibly removed over time. For an updated overview, you can refer to `https://docs.microsoft.com/en-us/azure/active-directory/develop/msal-overview`.

There are multiple ways in which tokens can be retrieved using MSAL. MSAL provides the following benefits for your applications:

- By using MSAL, there is no need to directly use OAuth code against the protocols or libraries in your application.

- Tokens can be acquired on behalf of a user or on behalf of an application (depending on the platform).

- Additionally, MSAL maintains a token cache and refreshes the tokens for you automatically when they expire.

- MSAL helps you to specify which type of audience you want to use to sign in to your application. This can be your own organization or tenant, multiple organizations or tenants, work or school accounts, Microsoft personal accounts, social identities using Azure AD B2C, or users in national and sovereign clouds.

- It provides functionality to troubleshoot apps and APIs. It does this by offering logging, telemetry, and actionable exceptions.

I highly recommend using both MSAL and the Microsoft Identity Web authentication library (for ASP.NET Core) for your applications. By using these libraries, Microsoft can ensure that your applications and APIs are secure from an identity and access management perspective. This is something that is a mandatory requirement in today's software development and is also difficult to implement in a secure manner on your own. It also takes away a lot of the complexity involved in acquiring and refreshing tokens.

After covering MSAL, we will implement some of the topics that we have covered so far in a demo. In the next section, we will build an application and secure it using OAuth 2.0, OpenID Connect, and MSAL.

Securing your application using OAuth 2.0, OpenID Connect, and MSAL

In the previous sections of this chapter, we covered the different frameworks for authenticating your applications in depth. In this section, we are going to put this learning into practice. We are going to build an ASP.NET Core web application that is going to use OAuth 2.0, OpenID Connect, and MSAL to authenticate a user against Azure AD and call the Microsoft Graph API.

This demo is going to be divided into two parts. The first part is going to cover the OAuth 2.0, OpenID Connect, and MSAL aspects. The second part is going to focus on the Graph API. The second part is going to be covered in *Chapter 6, Building Secure Services Using the Microsoft Graph API*.

In the first section of this demo, we are going to register the necessary applications in Azure AD and set the required permissions. However, we are going to do this manually. Since we have already covered this part in previous chapters, there is a PowerShell script available in the GitHub repository that can be used to automate this step.

In the following diagram, you can see the scenario that we are going to build in this demo:

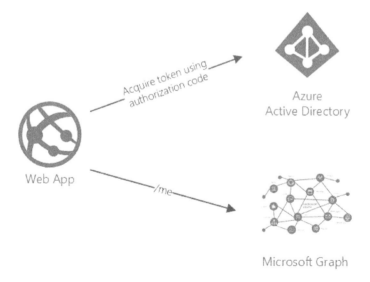

Figure 5.10 – The demo scenario

In this chapter, we are going to focus on the top part of the preceding diagram. Here, we going to set up Azure AD and build a web app that is going to leverage OAuth 2.0, OpenID Connect, and MSAL to sign in a user using a work or school account in Azure AD. In *Chapter 3, Application Types and User Consent*, we already covered some parts of this. However, in this chapter, we are going to build the application all by ourselves and walk through it in depth.

Registering the application with your Azure AD tenant

In the first step of this demo, we are going to register the applications in Azure AD. To do this, perform the following steps:

1. Open a web browser and navigate to `https://portal.azure.com`.

2. If you have multiple tenants, use the **Directory + subscription filter** option in the top-right menu to select the tenant where you want to register the application.

3. In the **Overview** page of Azure, select **Azure Active Directory**. Alternatively, type `Azure Active Directory` into the search box.

4. In the **Azure Active Directory** overview page, under **Manage**, select **App registrations**. Then, select **+ New registration**.

5. In the **App registration** blade, add the following values:

   - **Name**: `PacktWebApp`.

   - **Supported account types**: Only accounts that are in this organizational directory (we are going to use a work or school account that has been added to the Azure AD tenant).

   - **Redirect URI**: Select **Web** and add `https://localhost:44321/`.

6.   Click on **Register**:

Register an application ···

* Name

The user-facing display name for this application (this can be changed later).

> PacktWebApp   ✓

Supported account types

Who can use this application or access this API?

(•) Accounts in this organizational directory only (SZaal only - Single tenant)

◯ Accounts in any organizational directory (Any Azure AD directory - Multitenant)

◯ Accounts in any organizational directory (Any Azure AD directory - Multitenant) and personal Microsoft accounts (e.g. Skype, Xbox)

◯ Personal Microsoft accounts only

Help me choose...

Redirect URI (optional)

We'll return the authentication response to this URI after successfully authenticating the user. Providing this now is optional and it can be changed later, but a value is required for most authentication scenarios.

| Web   ∨ | https://localhost:44321/   ✓ |

Register an app you're working on here. Integrate gallery apps and other apps from outside your organization by adding from Enterprise applications.

By proceeding, you agree to the Microsoft Platform Policies ↗

> Register

Figure 5.11 – Registering the web app in Azure AD

7.   After the registration process is complete, copy the app ID and the directory tenant ID. Later in this demo, these IDs will need to be added to the configuration file of the application.

8.   Next, we need to configure the redirect URI for the web app. In the **App registration** blade, under **Manage**, select **Authentication**.

9.   Enter the following redirect URI in the **Redirect URIs** section: `https://localhost:44321/signin-oidc`.

10.   Add the following URL to the **Front-channel logout URL** section: `https://localhost:44321/signout-oidc`.

11.   In the **implicit grant and hybrid flows section**, enable **ID Tokens** for this application.

12. Click on **Save**:

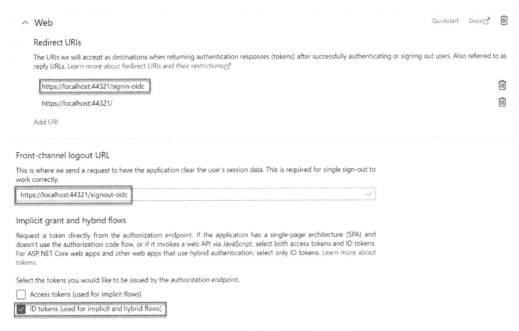

Figure 5.12 – Configuring the URIs

13. In the **App registration** blade, under **Manage**, select **Certificates & secrets**. Add a new client secret in the **Client secret** section by clicking on **+ New client secret**. Add the following values:

- **Description**: Packt app secret

- **Expires**: 6 months

14. Click on **Add**:

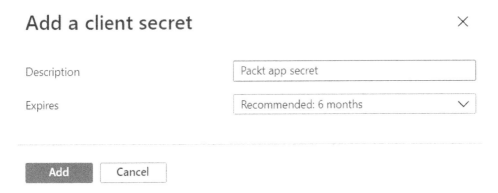

Figure 5.13 – Adding a client secret

15. Copy the secret value and paste it into the notepad.

16. Now, we need to add permissions to call the Microsoft Graph API. In most scenarios, these permissions are added automatically. If not, you need to add them manually. If they need to be added manually, in the **App registration** blade, under **Manage**, select **API Permissions**. Click on **+ Add a permission**:

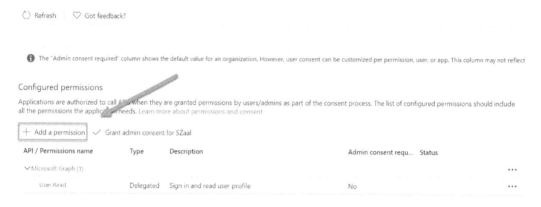

Figure 5.14 – Adding a permission

17. Ensure that the **Microsoft** tab has been selected, and then select the **Microsoft Graph** API:

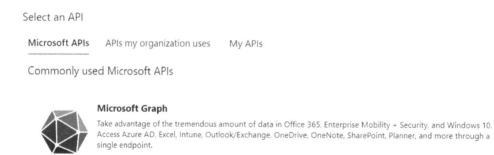

Figure 5.15 – Adding permissions

18. If it is not added automatically, select **Delegated permissions**. Under the **User** tab, select **User.Read** and click on **Add permissions**.

Now we have registered the web app and configured the redirect URIs, created an app secret, and configured the permissions to make a request to the Microsoft Graph API. Next, we are going to build the web application.

Building the application

In this step of the demo, we are going to build the ASP.NET Core web application. This application will use the app registration of the previous step to sign in to Azure AD.

For this example, I'm going to use Visual Studio Code; however, you can also use Visual Studio. The application has also been added to the GitHub repository of this book, in the `Chapter 5` folder. The app is called `PacktWebApp-OpenIDConnect-DotNet`.

To build the app, proceed with the following steps:

1. Navigate to the directory where you want to create your application on your local filesystem. Then, create a new folder called `PacktWebApp-OpenIDConnect-DotNet`. Open the folder, right-click in the File Explorer canvas to open the context menu, and select **Open with Code**:

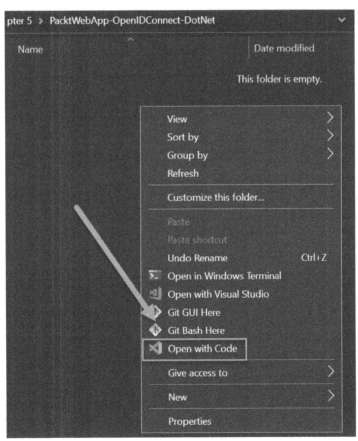

Figure 5.16 – Opening the web app folder in VS Code

2. Open a new Terminal by clicking on **Terminal | New Terminal** in the top-level window or by using *Ctrl + Shift + '*.

3. In the Terminal window, type in `dotnet new mvc`. The web app will be created using the **Model-View-Controller** (**MVC**) pattern.

4. First, we need to set the URL that the application will use when it is executed on the local filesystem. Open `launchsettings.json` in the `properties` folder and replace the code with the following:

```json
{
    "iisSettings": {
        "windowsAuthentication": false,
        "anonymousAuthentication": true,
        "iisExpress": {
            "applicationUrl": "http://localhost:3110",
            "sslPort": 44321
        }
    },
    "profiles": {
        "PacktWebApp_OpenIDConnect_DotNet": {
            "commandName": "Project",
            "dotnetRunMessages": true,
            "launchBrowser": true,
            "applicationUrl": "https://localhost:44321;http://
localhost:3110",
            "environmentVariables": {
                "ASPNETCORE_ENVIRONMENT": "Development"
            }
        },
        "IIS Express": {
            "commandName": "IISExpress",
            "launchBrowser": true,
            "environmentVariables": {
                "ASPNETCORE_ENVIRONMENT": "Development"
            }
        }
    }
}
```

5. Open the `appsettings.json` file and replace the `AzureAd` section with the following lines of code:

```
"AzureAd": {
    "Instance": "https://login.microsoftonline.com/",
    "Domain": "<Enter the domain of your tenant, e.g.
packt.onmicrosoft.com>",
    "TenantId": "<Enter 'common', or 'organizations' or
the Tenant Id>",
    "ClientId": "<Enter the Client Id (Application ID
obtained from the Azure portal>",
    "ClientSecret": "<Enter the client secret added to
the app from the Azure portal>",
    "ClientCertificates": [
    ],
    "CallbackPath": "/signin-oidc"
},
```

6. Replace the placeholders with the tenant ID, App ID, and the client secret based on the values from the app registration.

7. Next, we need to add the required NuGet packages to the project. Paste the following lines of code into a Terminal window:

```
dotnet add package Microsoft.Identity.Web
dotnet add package Microsoft.Identity.Web.UI
```

8. Now we can add the required code for authenticating the user to the project. Open `Startup.cs` and add the following `using` statements to the class:

```
using Microsoft.Identity.Web;
using Microsoft.Identity.Web.UI;
using Microsoft.AspNetCore.Authorization;
using Microsoft.AspNetCore.Mvc.Authorization;
using Microsoft.AspNetCore.Authentication.OpenIdConnect;
```

9. Next, replace the `ConfigureServices` method with the following:

```
public void ConfigureServices(IServiceCollection
services)
        {
            services.
AddAuthentication(OpenIdConnectDefaults.
AuthenticationScheme)
                .AddMicrosoftIdentityWebApp(Configuration.
GetSection("AzureAd"));

            services.AddControllersWithViews(options =>
            {
                var policy = new
AuthorizationPolicyBuilder()
                    .RequireAuthenticatedUser()
                    .Build();
                options.Filters.Add(new
AuthorizeFilter(policy));
            });
            services.AddRazorPages()
                .AddMicrosoftIdentityUI();
        }
```

10. In *Chapter 3, Application Types and User Consent*, we used the simplest form to sign in. We did this by only using the `services.AddMicrosoftIdentityWebAppAuthentication` method from the `Microsoft.Identity.Web` package. As you can see, in this example, we are doing things a little differently. We are using `Microsoft.Identity.Web` in conjunction with ASP.NET Core for integrating with the Microsoft identity platform.

11. In the `Configure` method, directly above `app.UseAuthorization();`, add `app.UseAuthentication();` and `endpoints.MapRazorPages();` to `app.UseEndpoints`.

12. Now we can run the application. Build and run the application. Sign in with a work or school account and accept the user consent form. The application will redirect you to the page that has been configured as the redirect URI.

We have now concluded the first part of this demo. In the next chapter, we will expand this application and add functionality to it to call the Microsoft Graph API on behalf of the signed-in user.

Summary

In this chapter, we covered OAuth 2.0, OpenID Connect, and MSAL in depth. We looked at the OAuth 2.0 specifications and flows. Then, we covered how the different flows can be integrated within the Microsoft identity platform. Next, we covered the Microsoft Identity Web authentication library and MSAL, and we learned how your applications can benefit from them, by ensuring you can keep your users and your data safe. Finally, we put the theory into practice and built an application that leveraged the Microsoft Identity Web authentication library to authenticate a user in Azure AD.

In the next chapter, we are going to cover how you can build secure services using the Microsoft Graph API. We are going to look at the different APIs that Microsoft Graph provides, how it integrates with Azure and Microsoft 365, and how to build queries to retrieve data. Lastly, we are going to finish the demo that we started to build in this chapter and add the functionality to call the Microsoft Graph API on behalf of the signed-in user.

Further reading

For more information about the topics that were covered in this chapter, you can check out the following links:

- *Authentication vs. Authorization*: `https://auth0.com/docs/get-started/authentication-and-authorization`

- *Microsoft identity platform and OpenID Connect protocol*: `https://docs.microsoft.com/en-us/azure/active-directory/develop/v2-protocols-oidc`

- *Microsoft identity platform and OAuth 2.0 authorization code flow*: `https://docs.microsoft.com/en-us/azure/active-directory/develop/v2-oauth2-auth-code-flow`

- *Microsoft identity platform and OAuth 2.0 On-Behalf-Of flow*: `https://docs.microsoft.com/en-us/azure/active-directory/develop/v2-oauth2-on-behalf-of-flow`

- *Microsoft identity platform and the OAuth 2.0 client credentials flow*: `https://docs.microsoft.com/en-us/azure/active-directory/develop/v2-oauth2-client-creds-grant-flow`

- *Microsoft identity platform and OAuth 2.0 Resource Owner Password Credentials*: `https://docs.microsoft.com/en-us/azure/active-directory/develop/v2-oauth-ropc`

- *Microsoft identity platform and the OAuth 2.0 device authorization grant flow*: `https://docs.microsoft.com/en-us/azure/active-directory/develop/v2-oauth2-device-code`

6
Building Secure Services Using the Microsoft Graph API

In the previous chapter, we covered OAuth 2.0, OpenID Connect, and the **Microsoft Authentication Library** (**MSAL**) in great depth. We looked at the different specifications and flows and authentication libraries that Microsoft provides. Then, we put the theory into practice and built an application that leverages the Microsoft Identity Web authentication library.

In this chapter, we are going to look, in depth, at the Microsoft Graph API. We are going to look at the different APIs that Microsoft Graph provides, how it integrates with Azure and Microsoft 365, and how to build queries to retrieve data. Finally, in this chapter, we are going to finish the demonstration that we are building and add some functionality to call the Microsoft Graph API on behalf of the signed-in user.

In this chapter, the following topics will be covered:

- An overview of Microsoft Graph

- Accessing data and methods

- Queries, batching, and throttling

- The Microsoft Graph SDK

- Building a web application that uses the Microsoft Graph API

Technical requirements

To follow this chapter, you need to have an active Azure Active Directory tenant. An Azure Active Directory tenant was created in *Chapter 1*, *Microsoft Identity Platform Overview*. Additionally, you will need to have the latest version of Visual Studio or Visual Studio Code installed:

- Visual Studio Code: `https://code.visualstudio.com/`

- Visual Studio: `https://visualstudio.microsoft.com/`

For the example in this chapter, I'm going to use Visual Studio Code, but of course, you can use Visual Studio, too.

You can download the source code of this chapter here: `https://github.com/PacktPublishing/Azure-Active-Directory-for-Developers/tree/main/Chapter%206`

An overview of Microsoft Graph

Microsoft Graph consists of a set of APIs that is provided by Microsoft to access data from Microsoft 365, acting as the gateway to data and intelligence. Microsoft 365 is a suite of different applications, such as Word, Excel, PowerPoint, Microsoft Teams, Outlook, and OneDrive. These services are offered to consumers and enterprises using a subscription model. Besides the office suite that it provides, there are also additional services around identity and access management, device and app management, files and content, advanced analytics, threat protection, and security and compliance management. On top of that, there are also plans in which an operating system such as Windows 11 is added.

> **Note**
>
> For a complete overview of all the different plans, features, and services, you can refer to the Microsoft 365 product site at `https://www.microsoft.com/en-us/microsoft-365/compare-microsoft-365-enterprise-plans`.

Microsoft Graph acts as the API gateway to access data from all of these different applications and services. Additionally, it provides developers with a unified programmability model to access data from Microsoft 365, Enterprise Mobility and Security, and Windows. To access the data from these products, Microsoft Graph offers three different features:

- **The Microsoft Graph API**: This is a single endpoint that can be used to access data from Microsoft 365, Enterprise Mobility and Security, and Windows. There are the provided REST APIs and SDKs that can be used in applications and services to securely access the single endpoint (`https://graph.microsoft.com`).

- **Microsoft Graph connectors**: All Microsoft 365 data is indexed by Microsoft Search. This makes the data searchable for users. With Microsoft Graph connectors, it is also possible to integrate data from external resources, for example, various Azure resources such as Azure SQL, Azure Data Lake, and Azure DevOps. Additionally, there is support for third-party services such as Service Now, Salesforce, Oracle, and more. Besides the connectors that are provided by Microsoft and other third parties, developers can build their own connectors.

- **Microsoft Graph Data Connect**: This service is meant for developing applications that use large amounts of data for intelligence, analytics, and business process optimization. It stores data from Microsoft 365 in Azure using Azure Data Factory. For instance, you can extract data at scale using Microsoft Graph Data Connect and then store it in an Azure storage service. Following this, you can train machine learning models using the data and provide stakeholders with an application that displays the outcome.

In the following diagram, you can see an overview of how Microsoft Graph connects to Microsoft 365 and Azure using the different features and services that it provides:

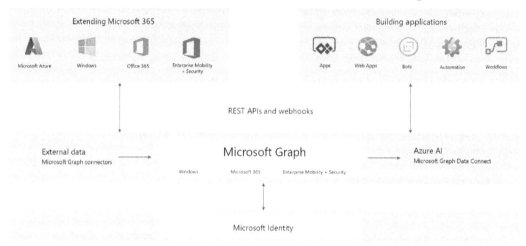

Figure 6.1 – An overview of Microsoft Graph

At the core, Microsoft Graph starts with users and groups. Around these users and groups, you can access data from the various Microsoft products that are included. Microsoft Graph builds a network around the user and accesses the data while protecting the user and the data with the necessary and configured authorization.

Microsoft Graph is a collection service that can be requested over a REST endpoint. The Microsoft Graph API defines most of its methods, resources, and enumerations in the OData namespace, which is called `microsoft.graph`. At first, Microsoft Graph included various services to access data coming from Office 365. Later, standalone REST APIs such as **Azure Active Directory** (**Azure AD**), Graph, and various other Azure APIs were integrated with the goal to provide a single endpoint for developers to access data from all different services and products.

> **Note**
>
> For an overview of all the services that are part of Microsoft Graph, you can refer to the official documentation at `https://docs.microsoft.com/en-us/graph/overview-major-services`.

Microsoft Graph is a REST API; this means that it can be accessed by every developer, using every programming language, framework, and platform. The only requirement is that the application or platform should be capable of making HTTP requests and then processing the responses that come from that request. Nowadays, all frameworks, platforms, and languages support these requirements. Microsoft Graph uses **Open DataProtocol** (**OData**) for RESTful API communications, which provides an open protocol to create and consume REST APIs in a simple and standard way. This is also used and supported in SharePoint, SAP, SQL Server, and many other technologies.

Additionally, Microsoft Graph provides multiple SDKs that can be used by developers in their code files and applications. These SDKs really simplify the interaction with Microsoft Graph, and they come with built-in security. Microsoft Graph supports two different types of authentications: work or school accounts and Microsoft accounts. For both, it uses Azure AD for authenticating the user.

Microsoft Graph provides two different service endpoints: the **v1.0** endpoint and the **beta** endpoint. All new features of Microsoft Graph are first made available in the beta version of the service. By using this service, developers can get early access to all of the new features. However, it is not recommended that you use this endpoint for production applications because updates are regularly pushed to the beta version. These updates can then break your application.

In this section, we briefly covered the different services of Microsoft Graph. In the next section, we are going to cover the different features that are available for developers, starting with how to access data and methods using Microsoft Graph.

Accessing data and methods

Microsoft Graph provides a REST endpoint to read and write data from multiple products and services. In addition to that, developers can also use a number of request patterns to query data and traverse through the different resources that Microsoft Graph provides. The metadata document that is provided as one of the resources can help developers to understand the data model, along with the various resources and the relationships between them.

The Microsoft Graph API metadata

The Microsoft Graph API metadata document is published at the service root level of the API. It can be reviewed using the following URLs (for both the v1.0 endpoint and the beta endpoint):

- `https://graph.microsoft.com/v1.0/$metadata`

- `https://graph.microsoft.com/beta/$metadata`

You can use the metadata endpoint to learn about the relationships between different entities that are present in Microsoft Graph. Additionally, you can learn more about how to establish the different URLs that navigate between the different entities. By making this request to Microsoft Graph, you can understand its data model, which also includes the different entity types, complex types (which are keyless), and enumerations that make up the different resources of Microsoft Graph. Most of the services are defined in the `microsoft.graph` OData namespace, but the metadata endpoint also supports how to define types, methods, and enumerations in parallel namespaces.

In the next section, we are going to take a look at the metadata endpoint using Graph Explorer.

Requesting data using Graph Explorer

We are going to test this call using **Graph Explorer**, an open source project that can be used as a prototyping tool to fulfill different types of app scenarios. You can easily make requests to Microsoft Graph and see the responses that are returned. It provides helpful features such as code snippets in various languages, for example, C#, JavaScript, Java, and more. Additionally, it provides sample queries that can be used and links to the official documentation for the sample queries.

To access the metadata document of the Graph API, perform the following steps:

1. Open a new browser window and navigate to `https://developer.microsoft.com/en-us/graph/graph-explorer`.

2. The Graph Explorer window will be displayed. In the following screenshot (*Figure 6.2*), you can see the web page for Graph Explorer, which includes the following elements:

    I.   **A sign-in button**: Here, you can sign in with your work or school account or your personal Microsoft account. You can use this account to build the network around the signed-in user and access the related data.

    II. An HTTP verb drop-down list to create the different types of REST API methods, such as GET, POST, PUT, PATCH, and DELETE.

III.   **The Graph API version selector**: Here, you can select whether you want to use the v1.0 endpoint or the beta endpoint.

IV.   **The request address bar**: Here, you can add the different types of requests that you want to make to the Graph API. By default, the /me endpoint is displayed here. This will give you information about the user, which is a sample user by default. After you sign in using an actual account, the information of the signed-in user will be queried using this request.

V.   This is one of the sample queries that is provided by Graph Explorer. There are more, which we will show later in this demonstration.

VI.   This is the documentation link that belongs to the sample query. Clicking on the button will redirect you to the corresponding documentation on the Microsoft documentation site:

Figure 6.2 – An overview of Graph Explorer

3. Let's make a request to retrieve the metadata document. First, sign in using a work or school account. Then, in the request bar, fill in the `https://graph.microsoft.com/v1.0/$metadata` URL. Click on **Run query** next to the request bar. By signing in with a user account, you will get a richer dataset in return when you run this request:

Figure 6.3 – The metadata document request and response

4. Take some time to discover the response of the metadata endpoint, as it is a huge list.

5. To view resources in a tenant, you can use HTTP GET queries. Let's try another basic request. This time, we will request a list of users. You can get the collection of user resources from a tenant. In Graph Explorer, we can make this request by selecting the GET query and adding the `https://graph.microsoft.com/v1.0/users` URL in the request bar. The bearer token, which we already covered in *Chapter 5*, *Securing Applications with OAuth 2.0, OpenID Connect, and MSAL*, is used to get access to the data of the tenant. This will be filled in automatically using Graph Explorer because we are already signed in as a user. It will use these credentials for creating an access token (bearer), which can then be used for making requests to the Graph API on behalf of the signed-in user.

6. Perform the following steps to get a response from the users:

   I.   Make sure you are signed in with a work or school account.

   II. Make sure that **GET** is selected in the REST API methods drop-down list.

   III. Add the following URL to the request bar: `https://graph.microsoft.com/v1.0/users`.

   IV. Click on the **Run query** button.

7. This will give you a `200 OK` response that looks similar to the following example. You will see the most common attributes of the different users that are present in the Azure AD tenant:

```json
{
    "@odata.context": "https://graph.microsoft.com/
v1.0/$metadata#users",
    "value": [
        {
            "businessPhones": [],
            "displayName": "SZ Demo1",
            "givenName": null,
            "jobTitle": null,
            "mail": "....@....com",
            "mobilePhone": null,
            "officeLocation": null,
            "preferredLanguage": null,
            "surname": null,
            "userPrincipalName": "..._....com#EXT#@....
onmicrosoft.com",
            "id": "b5b43768-n712-77kj-11c8-879dc34121475"
        },
        {
            "businessPhones": [],
            "displayName": "SZ Demo2",
            "givenName": null,
            "jobTitle": null,
            "mail": "....@....com",
            "mobilePhone": null,
```

```
            "officeLocation": null,
            "preferredLanguage": null,
            "surname": null,
            "userPrincipalName": "…_....com#EXT#@.....
onmicrosoft.com",
            "id": "2ac98720-f443-33c7-9216-35356484d1f0"
        }
    ]
}
```

8. In Graph Explorer, when you click on the **Access token** tab, you will see the access token that is generated for the signed-in user:

Figure 6.4 – The access token

Now that we have introduced Graph Explorer, made a request for the metadata document, along with a very basic query, in the next section, we will focus on how to create different types of queries and do batching and throttling.

Queries, batching, throttling, and paging

In the previous demo, we already made a very basic request to the /users endpoint of Microsoft Graph. Now we will focus on some different types of queries and also learn how to do batching and throttling.

Let's start with some queries that you can create in the next section.

Queries

You can create all sorts of queries using various endpoints in the Microsoft Graph API. Let's make a request to retrieve all of the different mail folders that the signed-in user has access to. For this, we are going to use the `/mailfolders` endpoint:

1. Make sure you are signed in using the preferred user account. Then, make sure the **GET REST API** method is selected. Add the following URL to the request bar: `https://graph.microsoft.com/v1.0/me/mailfolders`.

2. Click on **Run query**. The response will look similar to the following example:

```
{
    "@odata.context": "https://graph.microsoft.com/
v1.0/$metadata#users('15484228-64yt6-32e9-944c-
987876bc68d8aa')/mailFolders",
    "@odata.nextLink": "https://graph.microsoft.com/v1.0/
me/mailfolders?$skip=10",
    "value": [
        {
            "id": "AAMkADUyNzcxYWEyLWVhYzYtNDMxNi04MjFFhL…
            "displayName": "@Action",
            "parentFolderId":
"AAMkADUyNzcxYWEyLWVhYzYtNDMxN….",
            "childFolderCount": 0,
            "unreadItemCount": 0,
            "totalItemCount": 24,
            "isHidden": false
        },
        {
            "id":
"AAMkADUyNzcxYWEyLWVhYzYtNDMxNi04MjFhLTgwOWE5NmVjM…",
            "displayName": "@Archive",
            "parentFolderId":
"AAMkADUyNzcxYWEyLWVhYzYtNDMxNi04MjFhLTgwOWE5N…",
            "childFolderCount": 0,
            "unreadItemCount": 0,
            "totalItemCount": 0,
            "isHidden": false
        },
```

```json
            {
                "id":
    "AAMkADUyNzcxYWEyLWVhYzYtNDMxNi04MjFhLTg...
                "displayName": "@Read-Review",
                "parentFolderId":
    "AAMkADUyNzcxYWEyLWVhYzYtNDMxNi04MjFhLTgwO...",
                "childFolderCount": 0,
                "unreadItemCount": 0,
                "totalItemCount": 6,
                "isHidden": false
            }
        ]
    }
```

3. Here, you see that the Mailfolders of the signed-in user are retrieved. At the top, you can also see that a query parameter is being used. It uses the ODATA $skip parameter, which sets the number of items to be skipped at the start of the collection.

In the next section, we are going to look at query parameters in more detail.

Query parameters

The Microsoft Graph API supports the OData system query options. These options are compatible with the OData V4 query language. In the following list, you will see a few examples of query parameters that can be used in GET operations:

- $top: By using this parameter, you will set the page size of the results. An example of this is /mailfolders?$top=2.

- $count: By using this parameter, you will retrieve the total number of resources that are coming from the response. An example of this is /me/messages?$top=2&$count=true.

- $filter: By using this, the results (rows) will be filtered. An example of this could be /users?$filter=startswith(givenName,'J').

- $format: By using this parameter, the results will be formatted to a certain media format. An example of this could be /users?$format=json.

- `$orderby`: By using this parameter, the results are ordered. An example of this could be `/users?$format=json`.

- `$search`: By using this parameter, the results will be returned based on the search criteria, for instance, `/users?$orderby=displayName desc`.

- `$select`: By using this parameter, you will filter certain properties (columns). An example of this is `/users?$select=givenName,surname`.

- `$expand`: By using this parameter, you can also retrieve related resources, for example, `/groups?$expand=members`.

> **Note**
>
> For more information about other query parameters that are supported by the Graph API, you can refer to the official documentation at `https://docs.microsoft.com/en-us/graph/query-parameters`.

Next, let's learn about batching.

Batching

When querying Microsoft Graph, in many cases, you might want to retrieve multiple types of information about a single user. For instance, you might want to have the user details, profile picture, email messages, and calendar items. Normally, you need to make multiple GET requests to the Microsoft Graph API to retrieve this data. You can make this a lot more efficient by using batching.

The Graph API supports JSON batching, which helps you to optimize your application requests by combining multiple queries to save network latency. You can combine up to 20 requests in a single JSON object.

In the next demonstration, we will use a sample query of Graph Explorer to create a batch request:

1. Open a browser window and navigate to `https://developer.microsoft.com/en-us/graph/graph-explorer` again.

2. Sign in with a work or school account.

3. In the left-hand menu bar of Graph Explorer, under **Sample queries**, click on **Batching** and then select the **POST perform parallel GETs** option:

Figure 6.5 – Batching a sample query

4. This will add the `https://graph.microsoft.com/v1.0/$batch` URL to the request bar and the following query to the request body:

```
{
    "requests": [
        {
            "url": "/
me?$select=displayName,jobTitle,userPrincipalName",
            "method": "GET",
            "id": "1"
        },
```

```
        {
            "url": "/me/messages?$filter=importance eq
    'high'&$select=from,subject,receivedDateTime,
    bodyPreview",
            "method": "GET",
            "id": "2"
        },
        {
            "url": "/me/events",
            "method": "GET",
            "id": "3"
        }
    ]
}
```

5. By executing this parallel GET query, you will retrieve data from the /me endpoint, such as the user's job title, the principal's name, along with message information that has been filtered by importance and only displaying the subject, receivedDateTime, and bodyPreview. Additionally, it will retrieve the events. Now run this query by clicking on the **Run query** button.

6. Now, you will receive a parallel response that looks similar to the following screenshot:

Figure 6.6 – The batching response

7. Next, click on **Combine a POST and a GET** in the sample query list. This will
    add a query using a combination of writes and reads, along with the following
    request body:

```json
{
    "requests": [
        {
            "url": "/me/drive/root/children",
            "method": "POST",
            "id": "1",
            "body": {
                "name": "TestBatchingFolder",
                "folder": {}
            },
            "headers": {
                "Content-Type": "application/json"
            }
        },
        {
            "url": "/me/drive/root/children/
TestBatchingFolder",
            "method": "GET",
            "id": "2",
            "DependsOn": [
                "1"
            ]
        }
    ]
}
```

8. First, the POST request creates a `TestBatchingFolder` folder in OneDrive and then requests this folder again. If you run this query, the result will look similar to the following screenshot:

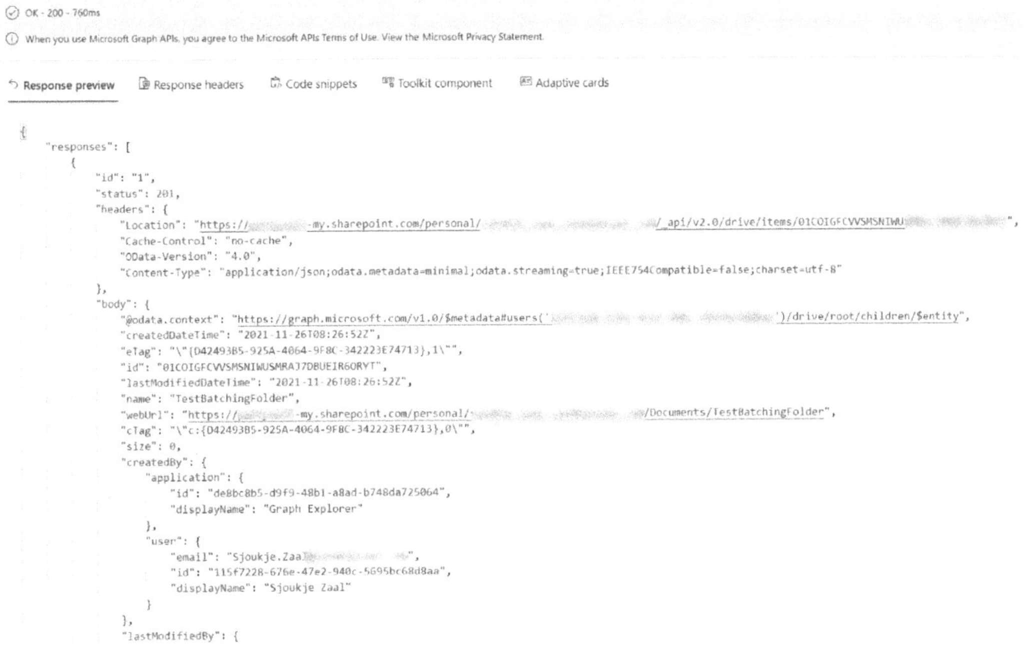

Figure 6.7 – Batching POST and GET responses

9. After running this query, open OneDrive, and you will see that the folder has been created there.

Now that we have covered how you can optimize your queries using batching in the Microsoft Graph API, in the next section, we will focus on throttling.

Throttling

Microsoft Graph is a public API that is exposed to everyone to call upon, and it is capable of handling a high volume of requests. However, all public APIs should have some sort of mechanism to limit the number of requests that can be made to protect them from applications calling too much data and consuming too many resources.

Additionally, Microsoft Graph has this kind of mechanism built in, in the form of throttling. If an overwhelming number of requests are made to Microsoft Graph, and the throttling threshold is exceeded, Microsoft Graph will limit any further requests from this specific client for a certain period of time. When this happens, the Graph API will return a status code of 429, which stands for too many requests. The request will then fail.

When the throttling threshold is exceeded, the Graph API will respond with the following:

```
HTTP/1.1 429 Too Many Requests
Content-Type: application/json
Retry-After: 1.218

{
  "error": {
    "code": "TooManyRequests",
    "innerError": {
      "code": "429",
      "date": "2021-11-26T09:50:23",
      "message": "Please retry after",
      "request-id": "94fb3d62-879a-2154-a601-43e1a76e1aa2",
      "status": "429"
    },
    "message": "Please retry again later."
  }
}
```

To handle throttling, it is important to reduce the number of operations that are sent per request to the Microsoft Graph API. It is also important to reduce the frequency of calls and avoid immediate retries. All requests will be added to the usage limits and logged by the Graph API. When you experience throttling, the response includes a Retry-After response header. Make a new request after this delay (in seconds) to retrieve the data from the Graph API again.

Now that we have covered some of the basics of Microsoft Graph, and how you can create sample queries using Graph Explorer, in the next section, we are going to cover the Microsoft Graph SDK.

The Microsoft Graph SDK

Having a well-built SDK is extremely important for developers. Not only will it make your life a lot easier, but it also handles security for you and increases the performance of your applications. It gives developers and users of your applications a consistent way of doing things.

This is also the case for Microsoft Graph. Microsoft provides the Microsoft Graph SDK, which has been specifically designed to simplify building applications that access Microsoft Graph. It includes two different components:

- **Service library**: This library consists of models and request builders that are generated from Microsoft Graph's metadata endpoint. When working with different datasets that are included in Microsoft Graph, this will provide a strongly typed and discoverable experience when writing your applications.

- **Core library**: The core library provides a set of built-in capabilities that help to implement common scenarios when working with the Microsoft Graph API. It offers support for authentication, retry handling, payload compression, and secure redirects. Also, it adds features for paging and creating batch requests.

The Microsoft Graph SDK is available for a wide range of languages and platforms. It is currently available for Android, Angular, ASP.NET Core and Framework, Go (Preview), iOS, JavaScript, Node.js, Java, PHP, PowerShell, Python, and Ruby.

Additionally, Microsoft offers a lot of documentation around this, alongside lots of code samples and tutorials on how to get started and how to build your first application. For instance, if we pick ASP.NET as an example, you will see that a lot of examples are provided, which you can use to start building your application:

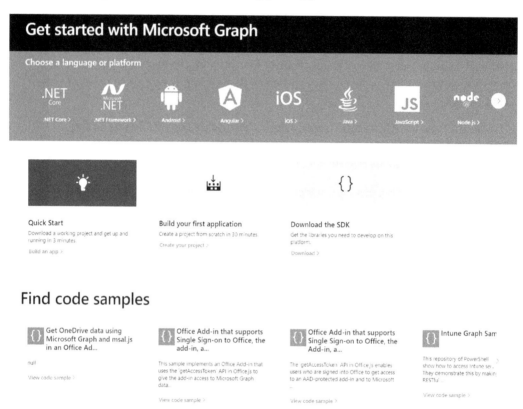

Figure 6.8 – Examples of the ASP.NET Microsoft Graph SDK

> **Note**
>
> These examples are also provided for the other languages and platforms. You can navigate to the Microsoft Graph SDK overview page at `https://docs.microsoft.com/en-us/graph/sdks/sdks-overview`. From there, click on your preferred language. You will then be redirected to the example website.

In the next section, we are going to use the Microsoft Graph SDK in our demonstration.

Building a web application that uses the Microsoft Graph API

In the previous sections of this chapter, we covered the features and capabilities of the Graph API. In this section, we are going to use the Graph API SDK to retrieve data from Microsoft 365.

This is the second part of this demonstration. We covered the first part in the previous chapter, where we focused on sign-in functionality using OAuth 2.0, OpenID Connect, and MSAL. In this second and last part, we are going to cover how to retrieve data from the Graph API using the credentials of a signed-in user.

If you need to set this application up from scratch, you can refer to *Chapter 5, Securing Applications with OAuth 2.0, OpenID Connect, and MSAL*. In the following diagram, you can see the scenario that we are going to build in this demo:

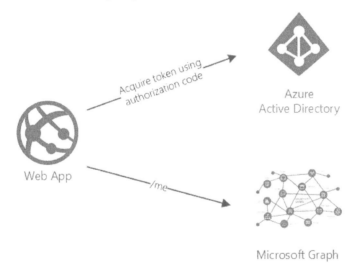

Figure 6.9 – The demo scenario

In this chapter, we are going to focus on the bottom part of the preceding diagram, where we connect to the Graph API and retrieve profile data for the user that is signed in to the application using a work or school account that has been registered in Azure AD.

To do this, perform the following steps:

1. Open the ASP.NET Core sample project, called `PacktWebApp-OpenIDConnect-DotNet`, that we created in the previous chapter in VS Code.

2. Open the `appsettings.json` file, and add the following lines of code underneath the Azure AD entry:

    ```
    "DownstreamApi": {
      "BaseUrl": "https://graph.microsoft.com/v1.0",
      "Scopes": "User.Read"
      },
    ```

3. This will set the Microsoft Graph URL to version 1 and add the scope to it. This scope corresponds with the scope that we configured in the previous chapter, where we registered and configured the application in Azure AD.

4. Next, we need to add the required NuGet packages to the project. Paste the following lines of code into a terminal:

    ```
    dotnet add package Microsoft.Identity.Web.MicrosoftGraph
    dotnet add package NewtonSoft.Json
    ```

5. Open the `Startup.cs` file. Then, replace `services.AddAuthentication` in the `ConfigureServices` method with the following:

    ```
                string[] initialScopes = Configuration.
    GetValue<string>("DownstreamApi:Scopes")?.Split(' ');
                services.
    AddAuthentication(OpenIdConnectDefaults.
    AuthenticationScheme)
                    .AddMicrosoftIdentityWebApp(Configuration.
    GetSection("AzureAd"))

      .EnableTokenAcquisitionToCallDownstreamApi(initialScop
    es)
                    .AddMicrosoftGraph(Configuration.
    GetSection("DownstreamApi"))
                    .AddInMemoryTokenCaches();
    ```

First, we need to get the scopes from the `appsettings.json` configuration file and add them to a variable.

The `AddMicrosoftIdentityWebApp()` method is used to sign the user in using the Microsoft identity platform endpoint. Using this endpoint, users can sign in using both a work or school account and a personal Microsoft account. In this demo, we are going to use a user that has been added to Azure AD using a work or school account.

Both `EnableTokenAcquisitionToCallDownstreamApi()` and `AddMicrosoftGraph` add support to the application to call the Microsoft Graph API. By using these lines in your code, you will ensure that the Graph API benefits from the optimized HTTP client management that has been built into ASP.NET Core. `EnableTokenAcquisitionToCallDownstreamApi()` adds the possibility of acquiring a token to call a protected web API using the scopes. Additionally, it enables controllers and pages to get `GraphServiceClient` using dependency injection and an in-memory token cache.

6. Next, open the `HomeController.cs` file from the `Controllers` folder.

7. Add the following `using` statements to the class:

```
using Microsoft.Identity.Web;
using Microsoft.Graph;
using System.IO;
```

8. Add the following code to the top of the class:

```
private readonly GraphServiceClient _graphServiceClient;
```

9. Next, replace the constructor with the following:

```
public HomeController(ILogger<HomeController> logger,
GraphServiceClient graphServiceClient)
    {
    _logger = logger;
    _graphServiceClient = graphServiceClient;
    }
```

10. We need to add some code to the `Index` method to make a request to Microsoft Graph and retrieve data from the `/me` API. Replace the `Index` method with the following:

```
public async Task<IActionResult> Index()
    {
        var user = await _graphServiceClient.
```

```
Me.Request().GetAsync();
        ViewData["ApiResult"] = user.DisplayName;

        return View();
}
```

11. We are going to create a `Profile` method that we can use to make a call to Microsoft Graph to retrieve the user's profile picture. Add the following code to the class, underneath the `Index` method:

```
[AuthorizeForScopes(ScopeKeySection =
"DownstreamApi:Scopes")]
        public async Task<IActionResult> Profile()
        {
            var me = await _graphServiceClient.Me.Request().
    GetAsync();
            ViewData["Me"] = me;

            try
            {
                // Get user photo
                using (var photoStream = await _
    graphServiceClient.Me.Photo.Content.Request().GetAsync())
                {
                    byte[] photoByte = ((MemoryStream)
    photoStream).ToArray();
                    ViewData["Photo"] = Convert.
    ToBase64String(photoByte);
                }
            }
            catch (System.Exception)
            {
                ViewData["Photo"] = null;
            }

            return View();
        }
```

12. Now, we also need a profile view to display the profile picture. In the `Views\Home` folder, add a new file called `Profile.cshtml`. We are going to add the code that adds the profile picture, which is coming from the Graph API. Therefore, add the following lines of code to it:

```
@using Newtonsoft.Json.Linq
@{
    ViewData["Title"] = "Profile";
}
<h2>@ViewData["Title"]</h2>
<h3>@ViewData["Message"]</h3>

<table class="table table-striped table-condensed"
style="font-family: monospace">
    <tr>
        <th>Property</th>
        <th>Value</th>
    </tr>
    <tr>
        <td>photo</td>
        <td>
            @{
                if (ViewData["photo"] != null)
                {
                    <img style="margin: 5px 0; width:
150px" src="data:image/jpeg;base64, @ViewData["photo"]"
/>
                }
                else
                {
                    <h3>NO PHOTO</h3>
                    <p>Check user profile in Azure Active
Directory to add a photo.</p>
                }
            }
        </td>
    </tr>
```

13. Next, we add the source code for retrieving additional user profile attributes from the Graph API and displaying them, too:

```
@{
        var me = ViewData["me"] as Microsoft.Graph.User;
        var properties = me.GetType().GetProperties();
        foreach (var child in properties)
        {
            object value = child.GetValue(me);
            string stringRepresentation;
            if (!(value is string) && value is
    IEnumerable<string>)
            {
                stringRepresentation = "["
                    + string.Join(", ", (value as
    IEnumerable<string>).OfType<object>().Select(c =>
    c.ToString()))
                    + "]";
            }
            else
            {
                stringRepresentation = value?.ToString();
            }

            <tr>
                <td> @child.Name </td>
                <td> @stringRepresentation </td>
            </tr>
        }
    }
</table>
```

This will retrieve the profile picture from Microsoft Graph and display it on the page. Additionally, it will iterate over all the other items that can be retrieved from the /me endpoint and also display these values on the page.

14. To get access to the profile page, we need to add a menu item. To do this, open the
    `_Layout.cshtml` file in the `Shared` library. Then, add the following line of code
    to the `navbar` div:

```
<li class="nav-item">
    <a class="nav-link text-dark" asp-area=""
asp-controller="Home" asp-action="Profile">Profile</a>
</li>
```

15. Make sure you have uploaded a picture in Azure AD for the account that you
    will use to sign in to the application. Now, run the application, sign in with a user,
    and in the top-level menu, select **Profile**. You will see an outcome similar to the
    following screenshot:

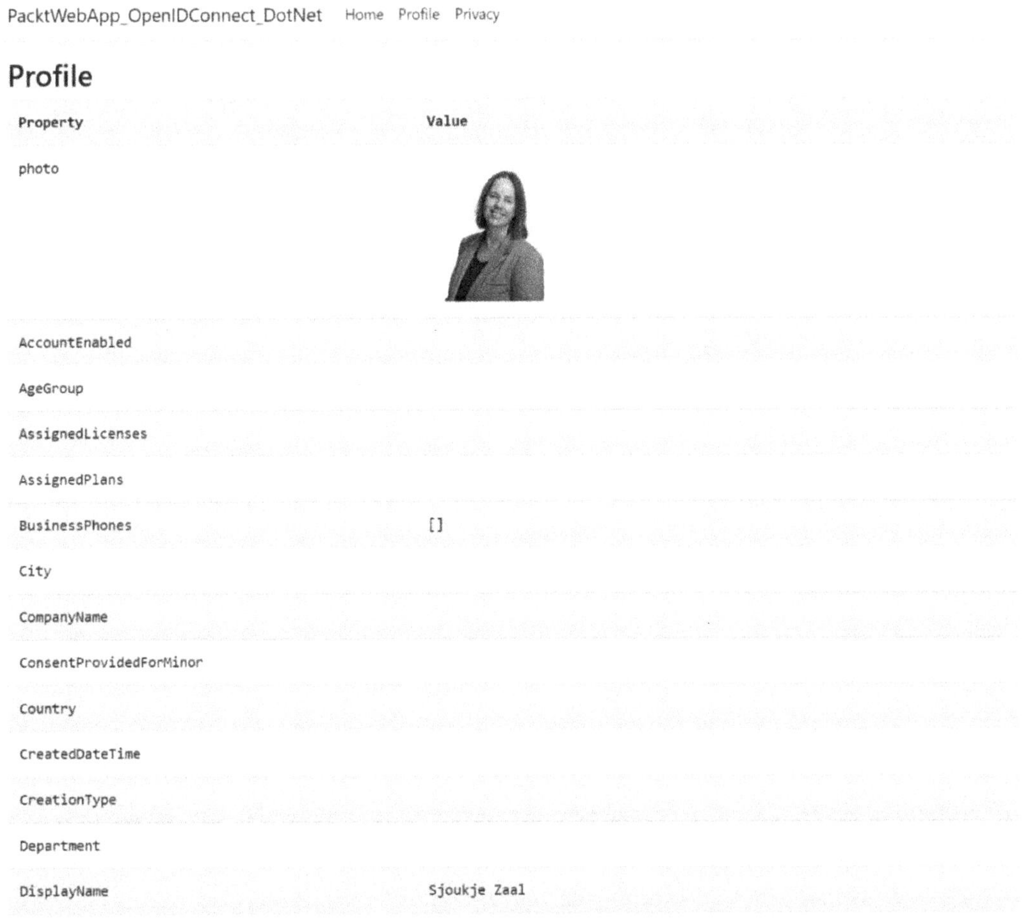

PacktWebApp_OpenIDConnect_DotNet   Home Profile Privacy

Profile

Property	Value
photo	
AccountEnabled	
AgeGroup	
AssignedLicenses	
AssignedPlans	
BusinessPhones	[]
City	
CompanyName	
ConsentProvidedForMinor	
Country	
CreatedDateTime	
CreationType	
Department	
DisplayName	Sjoukje Zaal

Figure 6.10 – The Profile page with Graph data

16. We have now retrieved the profile information for the user that is signed in using the Graph API.

This concludes the second part of this demo. In this demo, we built an ASP.NET Core MVC web application from scratch and added functionality for users to sign in using an account that is registered inside Azure AD. Then, we used OAuth 2.0, OpenID Connect, MSAL, and the Graph API to sign the user in and retrieve profile information from Azure AD using the /me endpoint of Microsoft Graph.

Summary

In this chapter, we covered Microsoft Graph in depth. We covered what features are provided by Microsoft Graph, such as the Graph API, the Microsoft Graph connectors, and Microsoft Graph Data Connect. Additionally, we covered how to create effective queries, how to do batching and paging, and how Microsoft Graph handles throttling. Next, we covered what tools and features Microsoft provides for developers to make life a whole lot easier by offering various SDKs. This provides a lot of built-in functionalities to retrieve data from the Microsoft Graph API in a secure and effective way.

This concludes Part 2 of this book. In the next part, we are going to cover Azure AD **Business-to-Consumer** (**B2C**). The next chapter will start by giving an overview of Azure AD B2C. We will cover how to create an Azure AD B2C tenant and add user accounts to it. Additionally, we will cover the different identity providers that are included in Azure AD B2C and how to set up out-of-the-box user flows and policies. Finally, we will look at how you can customize the UI for your signing-in and profile experiences in the Azure AD B2C tenants.

Further reading

You can check out the following links for more information about the topics that were covered in this chapter:

- *Microsoft Graph documentation*: https://docs.microsoft.com/en-us/graph/

- *Microsoft REST API Guidelines*: https://github.com/Microsoft/api-guidelines

- *Graph Explorer*: https://developer.microsoft.com/en-us/graph/graph-explorer

- *Microsoft Graph SDKs – Requirements and Design*: https://github.com/microsoftgraph/msgraph-sdk-design

Part 3: Azure AD B2C

In this last part of the book, we dive into Azure AD **Business to Consumer** (**B2C**) and how this can help developers secure their custom applications. We learn the basics, build applications that use Azure AD B2C as an identity provider, and finally examine the more advanced features of Azure AD B2C.

This part of the book comprises the following chapters:

- *Chapter 7, Introducing Azure Active Directory B2C*
- *Chapter 8, Advanced Features of Azure AD B2C*
- *Chapter 9, Azure AD B2C Custom Policies*

7

Introducing Azure Active Directory B2C

In the previous chapter, we covered Microsoft Graph in depth. We looked at queries, batching and paging, and how throttling is handled in Microsoft Graph. We finished the demo application that we started in *Chapter 5, Securing Applications with OAuth 2.0, OpenID Connect, and MSAL,* by using Microsoft Graph API to retrieve user profile information.

In the last part of this book, we are going to focus fully on Azure AD **Business to Customer** (**B2C**). In the first chapter, we are going to look at the built-in functionalities that Azure AD B2C has to offer. We are going to set up a B2C tenant and add a user to it. Next, we are going to cover user flows and policies and create a user flow with a template that comes with Azure AD B2C out of the box. And lastly, we are going to set up a web application that is going to authenticate against Azure AD B2C.

The following topics will be covered in this chapter:

- Introducing Azure AD B2C

- Creating an Azure AD B2C tenant and adding a user

- Registering an application in Azure AD B2C

- Understanding user flows

- Setting up the custom web application

Technical requirements

To follow along with this chapter, you need to have an active Azure subscription to create an Azure AD B2C tenant. You also need to have the latest version of Visual Studio or Visual Studio Code installed:

- Visual Studio Code: `https://code.visualstudio.com/`

- Visual Studio: `https://visualstudio.microsoft.com/`

I'm going to use Visual Studio for the example in this chapter, but of course, you can use Visual Studio Code as well.

You can download the source code of this chapter here: `https://github.com/PacktPublishing/Azure-Active-Directory-for-Developers/tree/main/Chapter%207`.

Introducing Azure AD B2C

Azure AD B2C provides a business-to-customer **Identity as a Service** in Azure. It mainly focuses on customer-facing websites and applications. It also offers functionality for customers to use their preferred accounts, such as local accounts, social accounts, and enterprise accounts. These accounts can then be used to acquire single sign-on access to your custom applications, websites, or APIs.

Both Azure AD and Azure AD B2C are specifically designed to scale. Both are capable of handling millions of users and billions of authentications per day. This scaling is completely handled by Azure, as well as the safety of the platform and monitoring. It also offers built-in support for protecting against brute-force attacks, handling threats such as **Denial-of-Service (DoS)**, and password spray.

Azure AD B2C is a completely separate service designed for a different purpose than Azure AD. It is aimed at developers and IT administrators who want to leverage a safe and secure authentication service that can be used for their customers. They can use different types of accounts to sign up or sign in, such as local accounts, which are stored directly in the Azure AD B2C directory, social media accounts, or enterprise accounts. Configuring different identity providers offers functionalities for your customers to sign up to your websites and applications by using their preferred accounts, with no restrictions. This is very different from what Azure AD has to offer, where users can only sign in using work or school accounts, and personal Microsoft accounts.

Azure AD B2C provides a directory that can hold up to 100 custom attributes per user. However, if your application or website is using an external identity provider, it is also possible to integrate Azure AD B2C with external systems. For instance, developers can use Azure AD B2C for authentication (using OAuth and OpenID Connect) but connect to a custom database or CRM system as the source of truth for customer data.

Azure AD B2C also offers built-in user flows that can be used by your customers to sign up, sign in, update profile information and passwords, and more. For this, it offers out-of-box templates that can be used, which can be configured inside the Azure AD B2C portal. This gives developers the ability to configure user flows without the need to make any changes to the code of the application. This provides huge flexibility; developers can change the user flows directly from the Azure AD portal, and all applications that use them are updated automatically. And besides out-of-the-box user flows, Azure AD B2C also offers the possibility to create custom user flows and policies to create more advanced flows for your customers.

> **Note**
> In this chapter, we will focus only on the built-in functionalities of Azure AD B2C. Custom user flows and policies will be covered in *Chapter 9, Azure AD B2C Custom Policies*.

Azure AD B2C is a white-label authentication solution. This means that it can seamlessly integrate with your custom applications. It can be embedded in your custom brand and the graphical design of your application without losing any of the authentication capabilities provided. The user flows, such as the sign-up, sign-in, password update, and reset flows, can be branded completely such that they fit into the design of your application or website by customizing the HTML, CSS, JavaScript, and more, of the user journeys. This way, the Azure AD B2C experience looks and feels like it is a native part of your application or website.

In the following diagram, you see an overview of the capabilities and functionalities in Azure AD B2C:

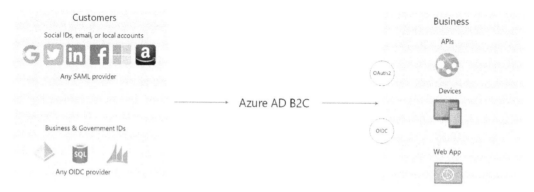

Figure 7.1 – Azure AD B2C overview

Now that we have some basic understanding of Azure AD B2C and the functionalities it has to offer, we are going to look at creating an Azure AD B2C tenant and how to add local accounts in the next section.

Creating an Azure AD B2C tenant and adding a user

Before we can get started with Azure AD B2C, we first need to create a tenant. As this is a separate product and not integrated with Azure AD, we need to create a separate tenant. We are also going to add the first user to the tenant manually. Therefore, you need to take the following steps:

1. Open a web browser and navigate to `https://portal.azure.com`.

2. We first need to add **Microsoft.AzureActiveDirectory** as a resource provider for the Azure subscription that you are using. In the search bar, search for `Subscriptions`. Select the subscription where you want to create the Azure AD B2C tenant and then, in the left menu under **Settings**, select **Resource Providers**.

3. Make sure that **Microsoft.AzureActiveDirectory** is registered. If it isn't registered, select the row and then select **Register**.

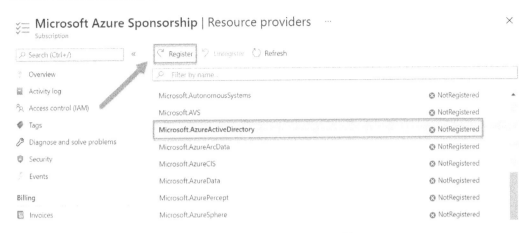

Figure 7.2 – Register resource provider

4. Next, go back to the home page of the Azure portal and click **+ Create a resource**. Type `Azure Active Directory B2C` in the search bar and then click **Create**.

5. Select **Create a new Azure AD B2C Tenant**.

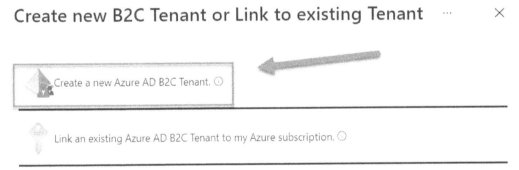

Figure 7.3 – Create a new Azure AD B2C tenant

6. Next, provide the following information to create the tenant:

- **Organization name:** `Packt B2C`.

- **Initial domain name:** Create a unique name here.

- **Country/Region:** United States.

- **Subscription:** Pick the subscription where you want to create the tenant.

- **Resource Group:** Create a new one and call it `packtb2c-rg`, for instance.

- **Resource group location**: West US.

Create a tenant ···   ✕

Azure Active Directory

* Basics   * **Configuration**   Review + create

Directory details

Configure your new directory

Organization name * ⓘ	Packt B2C ✓
Initial domain name * ⓘ	szpacktb2c ✓

szpacktb2c.onmicrosoft.com

Country/Region ⓘ	United States ⌄

✅ Datacenter location - United States

Datacenter location is based on the country/region selected above.
Azure Active Directory B2C service is available worldwide.

Subscription

Choose the subscription to use for Azure Active Directory (B2C). It's free for 50,000 monthly active users (MAUs).
See pricing details

Subscription *	Microsoft Azure Sponsorship ⌄
Resource group *	(New) packtb2c-rg ⌄
	Create new
Resource group location *	West US ⌄

[**Review + create**]   [< Previous] [Next : Review + create >]

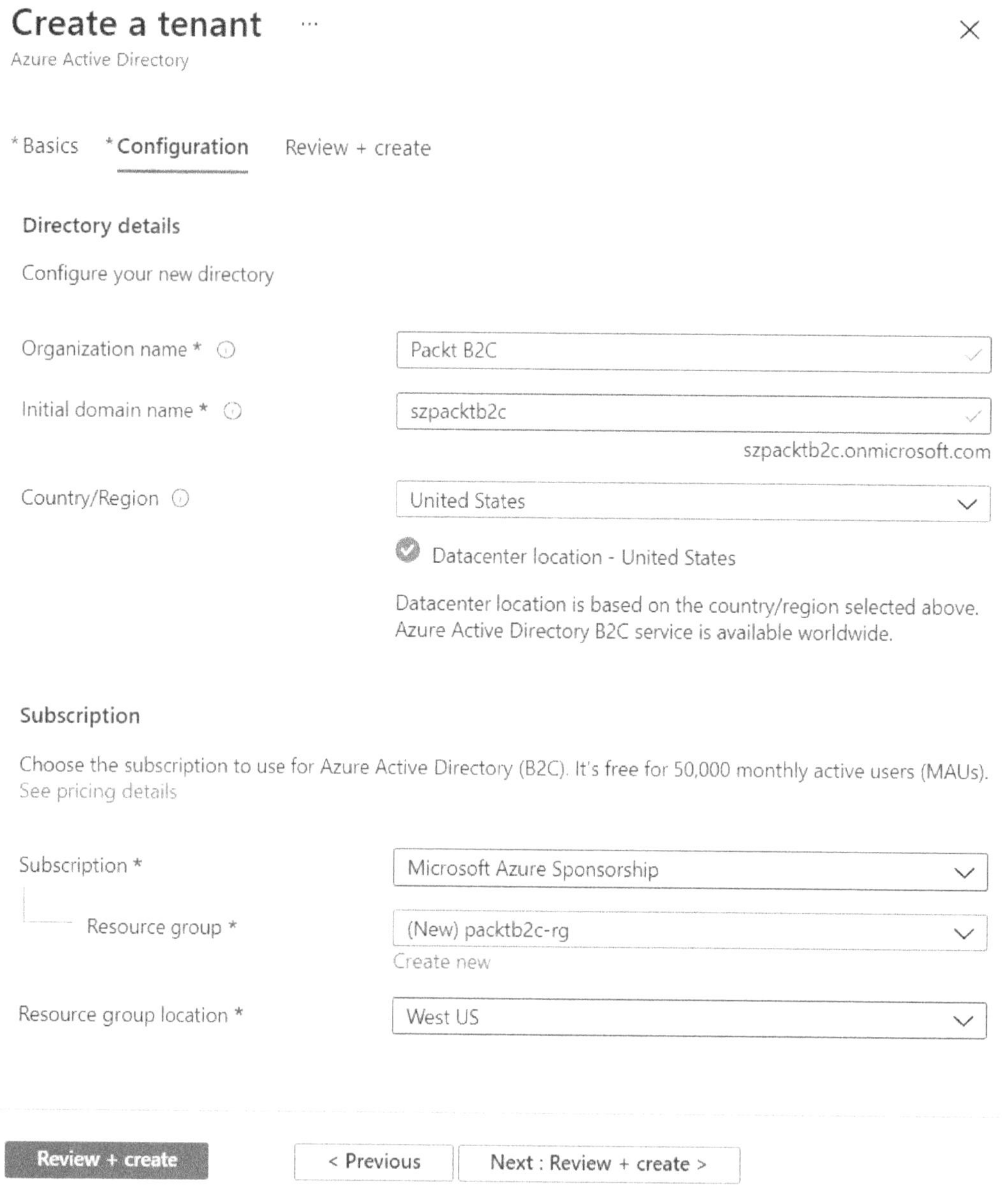

Figure 7.4 – Tenant details

7. Click **Review + create**.

8. When the validation passes, you can click **Create** to create the tenant. It can take some time before the tenant is created. After the tenant is created, a link will appear saying: **Tenant creation was successful. Click here to navigate to your new tenant: Packt B2C.**

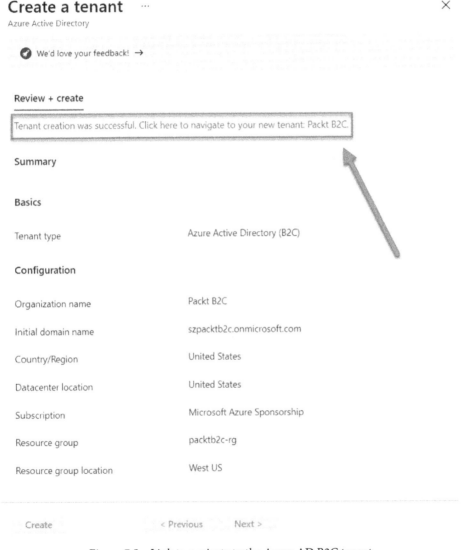

Figure 7.5 – Link to navigate to the Azure AD B2C tenant

9. Click the link to navigate to the newly created tenant. You will be asked to sign in again and afterward will be redirected to the tenant overview page of the Azure AD B2C tenant.

10. You can also switch between the different Azure AD tenants by clicking on the directories and subscriptions filter icon in the top menu bar.

Figure 7.6 – Directories and subscriptions filter icon

11. On the directories overview page, you can then select the Azure AD B2C tenant. Mine is already selected in this case.

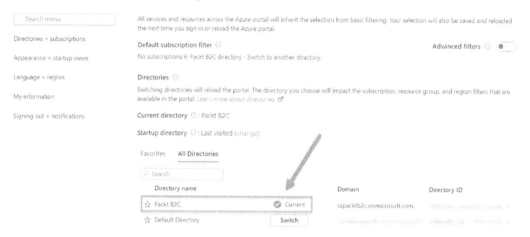

Figure 7.7 – Switch between Azure AD tenants

Now that we have created the Azure AD B2C tenant, we can add a local user account to it that is going to be stored directly in the Azure AD B2C directory:

1. In the Azure AD B2C tenant, in the left-hand menu under **Manage**, click **Users**.

2. You will notice that your account is already added to the tenant by default, with, in my case, **Source** as **Microsoft Account**. This is the same UI when you add a new user to an Azure AD tenant. Let's add an additional user. In the top menu, select **+ New user**.

Figure 7.8 – Adding a new user

3. In the new user blade, you will see that the **Create Azure AD B2C user** option is selected by default. Provide the following information for the new user:

    ▪ **Sign in method**: **Email**. Provide an email address here. I've used my Gmail account.

    ▪ **Name**: Provide your full name.

    ▪ **Block sign in**: **No**.

- Choose between an autogenerated password or create a password yourself. For this demo, I've used an autogenerated password. You can also show the password if you want to make a copy of it.
- Next, complete the **First name** and **Last name** fields.

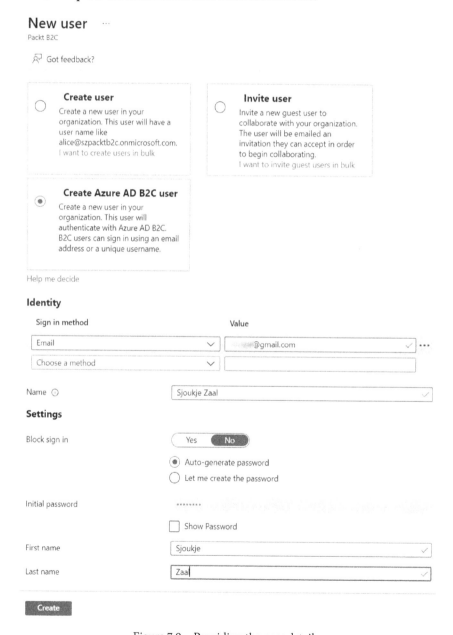

Figure 7.9 – Providing the user details

4. Click **Create**.

5. After creation, you will see that the source of this new user is **Azure Active Directory**. This user is created directly in the Azure AD tenant, which makes it a local user account.

This concludes the first demonstration. We created an Azure AD tenant and we have added our first local user. In the next section, we are going to look at how to register an application in Azure AD B2C.

Registering an application in Azure AD B2C

Similar to registering applications in Azure Active Directory, applications also need to be registered in the Azure AD B2C tenant before they can interact with Azure AD B2C. In this demonstration, we are going to register an application in it. Therefore, perform the following steps:

1. Open a web browser and navigate to `https://portal.azure.com`.

2. In the top-right menu, select **Directories + subscriptions** and make sure that the Azure AD B2C tenant we created in the previous step is selected.

3. Then, in the top search bar, search for `Azure AD B2C` and select it.

4. In the left menu, under **Manage**, select **App Registrations**. Then, in the top menu, click on **+ New registration**.

5. Add the following values to register a new application:

    - **Name**: `PacktB2Capp`.

    - **Supported account types**: Ensure **Accounts in any identity provider or organizational directory (for authenticating users with user flows)** is selected. This is the option that needs to be selected for Azure AD B2C applications.

    - **Redirect URI (recommended)**: Select **Web** and fill in `https://jwt.ms`. The authorization server, which, in this case, is Azure AD B2C, will redirect the application to this endpoint after completing the interaction with the user. The interaction consists of sending an access token or authorization code following successful authorization. We are using a Microsoft-owned web application for the redirect in this case. This website can be used for testing purposes and displays the decoded content of the token that is sent along. In production scenarios, you will use a public endpoint where the application is running, such as `https://packtpub.com/auth-response`.

- **Permissions**: Ensure that **Grant admin consent to openid and offline_access permissions** is selected.

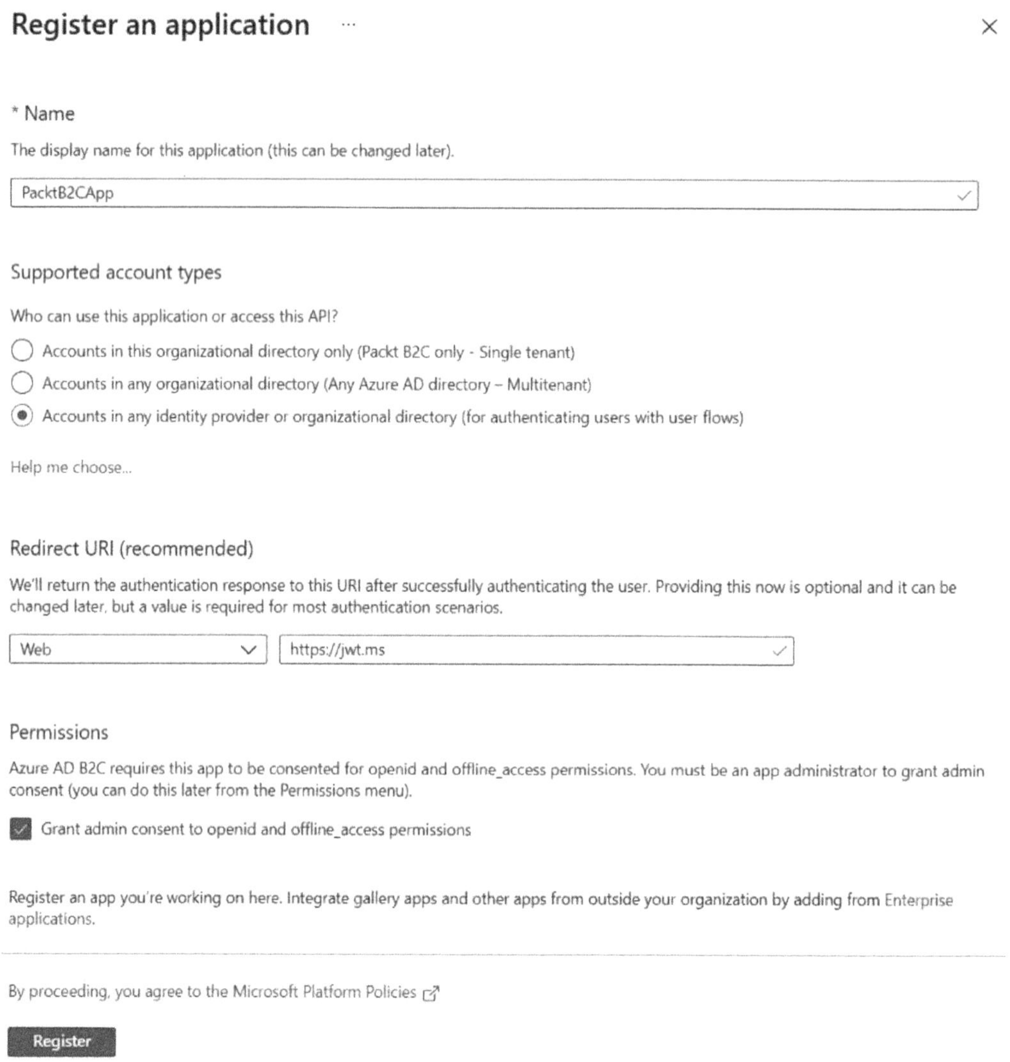

Register an application   ⋯   ✕

* Name

The display name for this application (this can be changed later).

PacktB2CApp   ✓

Supported account types

Who can use this application or access this API?

○ Accounts in this organizational directory only (Packt B2C only - Single tenant)

○ Accounts in any organizational directory (Any Azure AD directory – Multitenant)

◉ Accounts in any identity provider or organizational directory (for authenticating users with user flows)

Help me choose...

Redirect URI (recommended)

We'll return the authentication response to this URI after successfully authenticating the user. Providing this now is optional and it can be changed later, but a value is required for most authentication scenarios.

Web ∨		https://jwt.ms ✓

Permissions

Azure AD B2C requires this app to be consented for openid and offline_access permissions. You must be an app administrator to grant admin consent (you can do this later from the Permissions menu).

☑ Grant admin consent to openid and offline_access permissions

Register an app you're working on here. Integrate gallery apps and other apps from outside your organization by adding from Enterprise applications.

By proceeding, you agree to the Microsoft Platform Policies ↗

Register

Figure 7.10 – Registering an application in Azure AD B2C

6. Click **Register**.

7. On the **App registrations** overview page, copy the application ID and paste it in a notepad. We will need this when we are going to configure the application later in this chapter.

In the next section, we are going to take one last step, and that is to enable the ID token implicit grant.

Enabling the ID token implicit grant

The last step in this section is to enable the ID token implicit grant, which is also similar when registering applications in Azure AD. With implicit grant, the ID and access tokens are returned directly from Azure AD B2C to the application. For web applications such as ASP.NET MVC or ASP.NET Core (and also the `https://jwt.ms` website), we need to enable this. Perform the following steps:

1. From the **Certificates & secrets** overview page, in the left menu, under **Manage**, select **Authentication**.

2. Then, under **Implicit grant and hybrid flows**, select both the checkboxes.

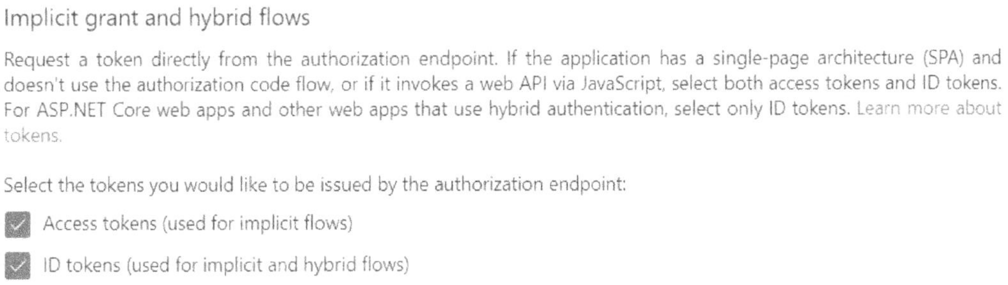

Implicit grant and hybrid flows

Request a token directly from the authorization endpoint. If the application has a single-page architecture (SPA) and doesn't use the authorization code flow, or if it invokes a web API via JavaScript, select both access tokens and ID tokens. For ASP.NET Core web apps and other web apps that use hybrid authentication, select only ID tokens. Learn more about tokens.

Select the tokens you would like to be issued by the authorization endpoint:

☑ Access tokens (used for implicit flows)

☑ ID tokens (used for implicit and hybrid flows)

Figure 7.11 – Enabling implicit grant and hybrid flows

3. Then, click **Save** in the top menu.

We have now registered an application in Azure AD B2C and set all the required configurations. In the next section, we are going to cover user flows and policies in Azure AD B2C.

Understanding user flows

With user flows and policies in Azure AD B2C, developers and administrators can set up complete user identity experiences. The business logic that users follow during these experiences can be configured in the Azure AD B2C tenant, directly from the Azure portal. When setting up a user flow, you can configure exactly which steps users will follow when users are signing up, signing in, resetting their password, and editing their profile in your custom application. When the experience is completed, the user will authenticate, and the app can acquire a token that gives the user access to your application.

Azure AD B2C offers two different ways to provide user experiences. The first is by using out-of-the-box user flows, which we are going to cover in this section. The other way is by creating custom policies. If you have requirements that are not provided by the built-in user flows, you can choose to build a custom policy. These are XML files that can be uploaded to the Azure AD B2C tenant and then used in your application as well.

> **Note**
>
> We are going to cover custom policies in *Chapter 8, Advanced Features of Azure AD B2C.*

Azure AD B2C provides the following out-of-the-box user flow experiences:

- **Sign up and sign in**: This flow type enables a user to create an account or sign in to their account.

- **Profile editing**: Enables a user to configure their user attributes.

- **Password reset**: This flow type enables a user to choose a new password after verifying their email.

- **Sign up**: This flow enables a user to create a new account.

- **Sign in**: Enables a user to sign in to their account.

- **Sign in using resource owner password credentials (ROPC)**: Enables a user with a local account to sign in directly in native applications.

These flow types can be configured in the Azure AD B2C tenant and can then be referred to from the application that uses them. This also means that changes to these flows can be made without the need to update the application code. These user flows also come with enterprise-grade security features, such as Azure AD **Multi-Factor Authentication (MFA)** and Azure AD Conditional Access policies. They will give you the ability to set the claims in the token that your application receives after the user completes the flow. These claims can then be used for authorization purposes in your application.

In the next section, we are going to create a sign-up and sign-in flow.

Creating sign-up and sign-in flows

In this demonstration, we are going to create sign-up and sign-in user flows. To do this, perform the following steps:

1. Open a web browser and navigate to `https://portal.azure.com`. Switch to the Azure AD B2C tenant again if required.

2. In the left menu, under **Policies**, select **User flows**.

3. In the top menu, click on **+ New user flow**.

4. This will open the **Create a user flow** blade. Select the **Sign up and sign in** user flow.

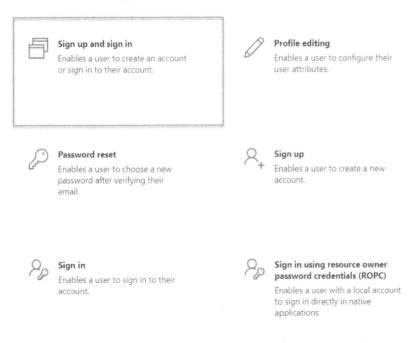

Create a user flow   ⋯

User flows are predefined, configured policies that you can use to set up authentication experiences for your end users. Select a user flow type to get started. Learn more.

Select a user flow type

Sign up and sign in Enables a user to create an account or sign in to their account.	**Profile editing** Enables a user to configure their user attributes.
Password reset Enables a user to choose a new password after verifying their email.	**Sign up** Enables a user to create a new account.
Sign in Enables a user to sign in to their account.	**Sign in using resource owner password credentials (ROPC)** Enables a user with a local account to sign in directly in native applications

Figure 7.12 – Sign up and sign in flow

5. Under **Version**, select **Recommended**. The user flows provided by Azure AD B2C have evolved over time. New versions have been released for the public cloud, which means that the legacy versions are deprecated.

Version

Figure 7.13 – Selecting the user flow version

> **Note**
>
> For more information about the user flow versions, you can refer to the Microsoft documentation: `https://docs.microsoft.com/en-us/azure/active-directory-b2c/user-flow-versions`.

6. Click **Create**.

7. In the **Create** blade, add the following values:

*   **Name**: `packtsignupsignin`.

*   **Identity providers**: Select **Email signup** (we are going to configure additional identity providers in *Chapter 8, Advanced Features of Azure AD B2C*).

*   **Multifactor authentication**: Keep the default settings here. It is extremely easy to set up MFA for your application in Azure AD B2C. It can be configured in its entirety here. You can set the type of method and the MFA enforcement.

- **Conditional access**: Here you can also configure conditional access policies. For this, it uses the conditional access policies from Azure AD. This means that you need a sufficient Azure AD license to use conditional access policies. Leave it unchecked here.

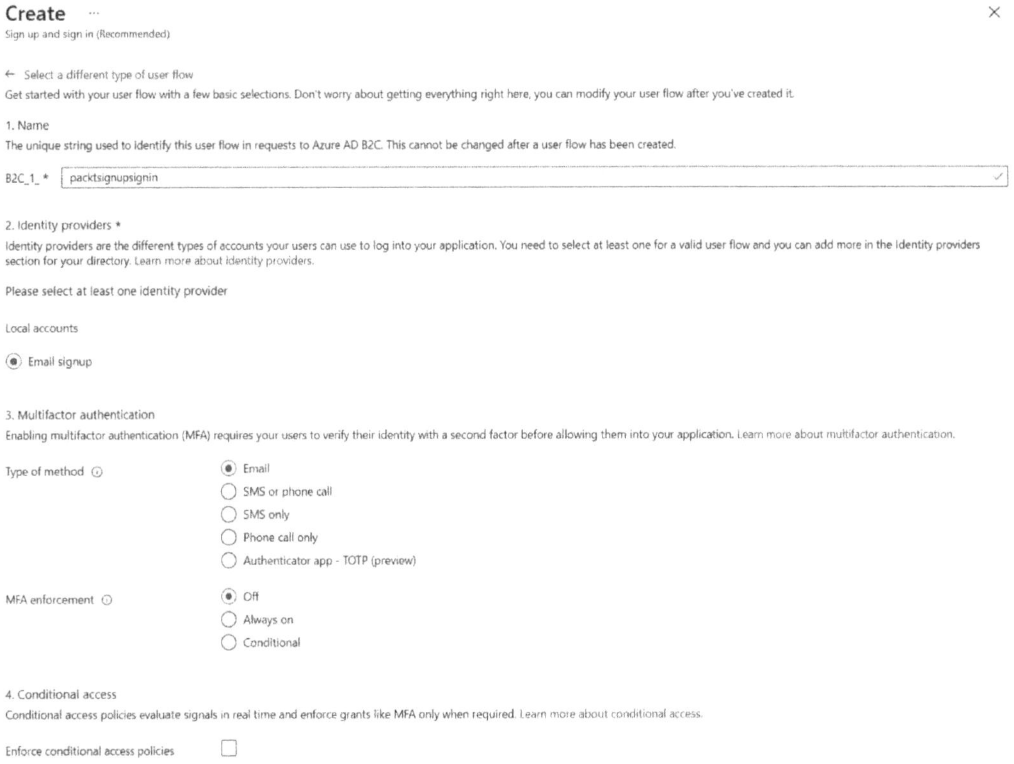

Figure 7.14 – Creating the user flow

- **User attributes and token claims**: Here you can choose the claims and attributes that you want to retrieve from the user during signup and return them to the application inside the token. Select **Show more…** and then select some user attributes here. I've selected **Country/Region**, **Display Name**, **Postal Code**, and **Street Address**. Select both the **Collect attribute** and **Return claim** checkboxes. The user will need to fill in these values during signup and then they will be sent along inside the token.

Figure 7.15 – Selecting user attributes and token claims

8. Click **Create**.

We have now created the sign-up and sign-in flows. In the next section, we are going to test this flow.

Testing the sign-up and sign-in flows

In the second part of this demonstration, we are going to test the user flow directly from the Azure portal:

1. From the **User flows** overview blade, select the user flow that we created in the previous step.

Figure 7.16 – Selecting the user flow

2. Here, you can change the settings for this flow. If you want to add additional identity providers after creation, or set different claims, you can do this from here. We are now going to test the flow. In the top menu, select **Run user flow**.

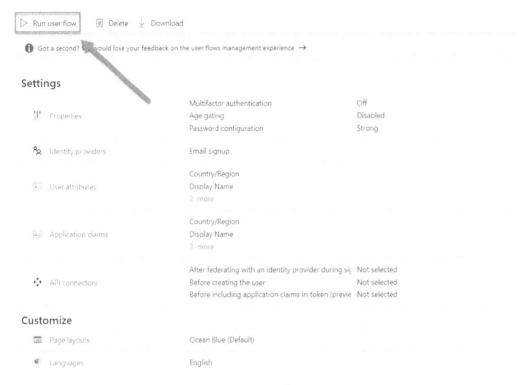

Figure 7.17 – User flow settings

3. Select the application that we have registered in the previous step. The **Reply URL** field should have https://jwt.ms. The endpoint should also be filled in automatically, referring to the Azure B2C tenant.

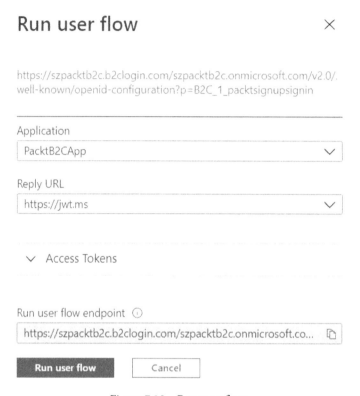

Figure 7.18 – Run user flow

4. Click **Run user flow**. This will open a new window with the default Azure AD B2C sign-up and sign-in experience, including the default graphical design. Here, select the **Sign up now** link.

Figure 7.19 – Sign-in and sign-up page

5. On the next page, you can sign up for a user account. Here, you need to provide an email address first. Then, click the **Send verification code** button. The verification code will be sent to the email address that you provide. Obtain the code, fill it in, and then click **Verify code**.

6. Now you can provide a password and confirm it.

7. You also need to specify the **Country/Region**, **Display Name**, **Postal Code**, and **Street Address** fields. Because we checked these boxes during the creation of the user flow, we now need to specify this information. This will be stored inside the Azure AD B2C tenant and will be passed on in the access token as well. Fill in the required information.

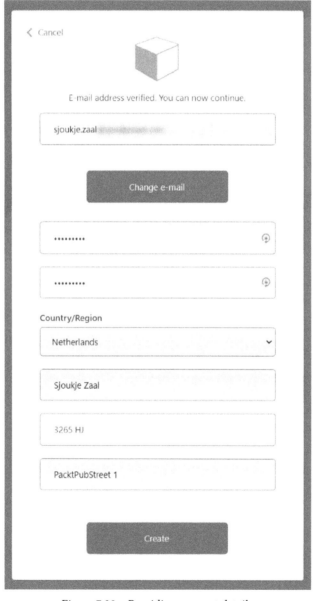

Figure 7.20 – Providing account details

8. Then, click the **Create** button to create the account inside Azure AD B2C.

9. You will now be redirected to the redirect URI (`https://jwt.ms/`) that we configure when we registered the application. Here, you can see the access token and also see the decoded token.

jwt.ms

Enter token below (it never leaves your browser):

eyJ0eXAiOiJKV1QiLCJhbGciOiJSUzI1NiIsImtpZCI6Ilg1ZVhrNHh5b2pORnVtMWtsMll0djhkNE5QNC1jNTdkTzZRR1RWQndhTmsifQ.eyJleHAiOjE2NDDA2ODK2NjEsIm5iZiI6MTY0MDY4NjA2MSwidmVyIjoiMS4wIiwiaXNzIjoiaHR0cHM6Ly9zenBhY2t0b2jJjLmIyY2xvZ2luLmNvbVS9kMzg4MDIwMy02MjJlLTQyMjktOWRkMC05M2VhZWNmZjZlZTDkdjIuMC8iLCJzdWIiOiI2NTM4ZTY2OS1jMWM4LTRhOTYtYTMzZC01MDdkZTc1NjQ2MzgiLCJhdWQiOiIxOWJjNDdmMi0yNWQ4LTQ0ZjMtODBmZi0yZmZiN2NjNjdkNzEiLCJub25jZSI6ImRlZmF1bHROb25jZSIsImlhdCI6MTY0MDY4NjA2MSwiYXV0aF90aW1lIjoxNjQwNjg2MDYxLCJjb3VudHJ5IjoiTmV0aGVybGFuZHMiLCJuYW1lIjoiU2pvdWtqZSBaYWFsIiwicG9zdGFsQ29kZSI6IjMyNjUgSEoiLCJzdHJlZXRBZGRyZXNzIjoiUGFja3RQdWJTdHJlZXQgMSIsInRmcCI6IkIyQ18xbnBnWc2lnbmluIn0.gXp4cQcdvMVLTvzjLxQHQoPRDntdI2-yH-kdsnHtzKJGR6YWz9lXEd3cDIrb8ggTFGMjICMPDzGGXloAnUrvG1nt9xO1-7LZIkvyqdFyCdTKOafggsKA1l9Mu2TgOYTsnjH-6hI7HhOQ9b9QwhEQQ44I_jY0dYpLCq_uNyT8V_BgkojPE-tHk8HKs5hKZzXLJh14iWnkxyJ-1iaCsGeN9lxujTJchMgJrmB3LTp35MZHMfvKtkMTCu68JtBUoTgKsSeaDW2Z_wgPKccYYsKKDmix5SIztYzJme1V7EHKuQrd4UzQk-GfqgZhA7SfR-gp8kkfZgqWk6wh5O4XSAmTsA

This token was issued by Azure AD B2C.

Decoded Token   Claims

```
{
  "typ": "JWT",
  "alg": "RS256",
  "kid": "X5eXk4xyojNFum1kl2Ytv8d1NP4-c57dO6QGTVBwaNk"
}.{
  "exp": 1640689661,
  "nbf": 1640686061,
  "ver": "1.0",
  "iss": "https://szpacktb2c.b2clogin.com/                              /v2.0/",
  "sub": "6538e669-c1c8-4a96-a33d-507de7564638",
  "aud": "19bc47f2-25d8-44f3-80ff-2ffb7cc67d71",
  "nonce": "defaultNonce",
  "iat": 1640686061,
  "auth_time": 1640686061,
  "country": "Netherlands",
  "name": "Sjoukje Zaal",
  "postalCode": "3265 HJ",
  "streetAddress": "PacktPubStreet 1",
  "tfp": "B2C_1_packtsignupsignin"
}.[Signature]
```

Figure 7.21 – Decoded token

10. You can run the user flow again. Now, sign in with the account that you just created. Then select **Claims**. The returned token will then include the claims that we configured in the user flow.

country	Netherlands	The country in which the user is located.
name	Sjoukje Zaal	The user's full name in displayable form including all name parts, possibly including titles and suffixes.
postalCode	3265 HJ	The postal code of the user's address.
streetAddress	PacktPubStreet 1	The street address where the user is located.
tfp	B2C_1_packtsignupsignin	This is the name of the policy that was used to acquire the token.

Figure 7.22 – Returned claims

We have now set up and tested the sign-up and sign-in user flows. In the next section and the final section of this chapter, we are going to set up the custom application that authenticates against Azure AD B2C and will use this user flow.

Setting up the custom web application

In the last part of this chapter, we are going to set up the web application. We are not going to build this application completely from scratch because this way we will repeat a lot of actions that we already did in the previous chapters. Setting up the application code for an application that authenticates against Azure AD B2C is similar to connecting an application to Azure Active Directory. They both use OAuth 2 and OpenID Connect, and the SDKs are the same as well. For this demonstration, we are going to use the sample application from the GitHub folder. The download link can be obtained from the *Technical requirements* section at the beginning of this chapter.

We will only make the required changes to connect to the Azure AD B2C tenant and add the correct user flow to web.config:

1. Download the sample code from GitHub and open the sample application in the chapter 7 folder.

2. Open the application in Visual Studio and open `appsettings.json`. Make the required changes to the following part of the code. Add the Azure AD tenant to `instance` and the `domain` entry. This can be retrieved from the Azure B2C tenant details in the Azure portal. Add `ClientID` (the client ID is the application ID that we copied to the notepad after registering the application in Azure AD B2C). Also, add the sign-up user flow name to it:

```json
{
    "AzureAdB2C": {
        "Instance": "https://<your-domain>.b2clogin.com",
        "Domain": "<your-domain>.onmicrosoft.com",
        "ClientId": "<web-app-application-id>",
        "SignedOutCallbackPath": "/signout/<your-sign-up-in-policy>",
        "SignUpSignInPolicyId": "<your-sign-up-in-policy>"
    },
```

This will look like the following screenshot:

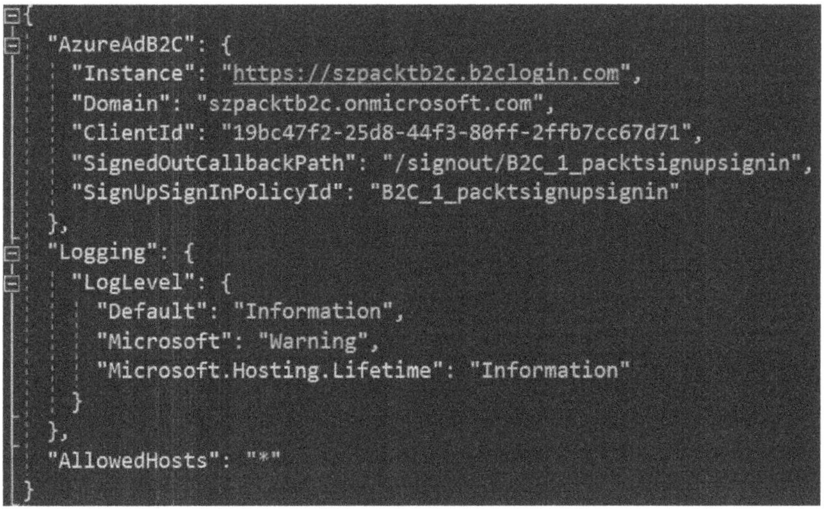

```json
{
    "AzureAdB2C": {
        "Instance": "https://szpacktb2c.b2clogin.com",
        "Domain": "szpacktb2c.onmicrosoft.com",
        "ClientId": "19bc47f2-25d8-44f3-80ff-2ffb7cc67d71",
        "SignedOutCallbackPath": "/signout/B2C_1_packtsignupsignin",
        "SignUpSignInPolicyId": "B2C_1_packtsignupsignin"
    },
    "Logging": {
        "LogLevel": {
            "Default": "Information",
            "Microsoft": "Warning",
            "Microsoft.Hosting.Lifetime": "Information"
        }
    },
    "AllowedHosts": "*"
}
```

Figure 7.23 – appsettings.json

3. Before we move on with the application, we first need to update the Redirect URI for the app registration in the Azure B2C tenant. Navigate to the Azure portal, search for `Azure AD B2C` in the search bar, and go to **App Registrations**. Click on the app registration, and in the left menu select **Authentication**. Add `https://localhost:44316/signin-oidc` (the sample application is configured to run on this port) to the **Redirect URIs** section and then click on **Save** in the top menu.

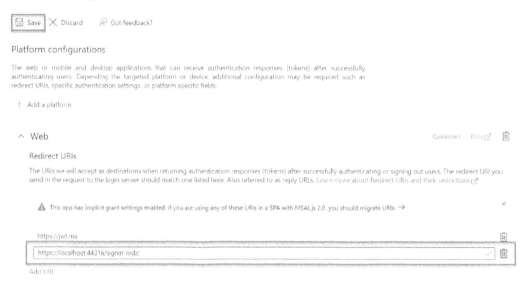

Figure 7.24 – Adding an application Redirect URI

4. Next, open `Startup.cs` in Visual Studio and, in the `ConfigureServices` method, scroll down to the part where the Microsoft Identity Web Authentication is called using the Azure AD B2C configuration config name:

```
// Configuration to sign-in users
with Azure AD B2C  services.
AddMicrosoftIdentityWebAppAuthentication(Configuration,
Constants.AzureAdB2C);
```

5. Scroll down a bit until you come to the part where the `appsettings.json` config values are added to the ASP.NET Core authentication library using OpenID Connect:

```
//Configuring appsettings section AzureAdB2C, into
Ioptions
services.AddOptions();
services.Configure<OpenIdConnectOptions>(Configuration.
GetSection("AzureAdB2C"));
```

6. These are the steps involved in letting your application authenticate to Azure AD B2C. And, as you have probably noticed by now, this is similar to applications that authenticate to Azure Active Directory. Only the `appsettings.json` config is a bit different because the user flows are added to it, and there are some small differences in the code because it refers to Azure AD B2C instead of Azure AD.

7. Now, let's execute this code. Press *F5* to build and run this application locally.

8. Click the **SignUp/In** button in the top-right corner.

Figure 7.25 – Sample web application

9. The default sign-in page of Azure AD B2C is loaded again. Sign up with a new user account or sign in using one of the accounts that are already added to Azure AD B2C. After successfully authenticating against Azure AD B2C, you will see your name in the top menu bar. This sample application also has a **Claims** page. Click on the link in the top menu.

Figure 7.26 – Signed in to the application

10. Here you can check the claims that are sent inside the access token.

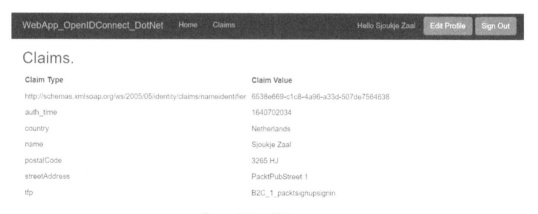

Figure 7.27 – Claims page

This concludes this demonstration and this chapter. We have now successfully authenticated against Azure AD B2C using an ASP.NET Core application.

Summary

In this chapter, we have focused on Azure AD B2C. We have covered what features and functionalities Azure AD B2C has to offer, and we created a tenant, registered an application in it, and created a user flow. Finally, we used a sample application to connect to Azure AD and the configured app registration and signed in with a user account added to the Azure AD tenant.

In the next chapter, will continue with Azure AD B2C and we will build upon the demos that we created in this chapter. In the next chapter, we are going to focus on identity providers in Azure AD B2C and we will create a custom policy that sends data from Azure AD B2C to an Azure function when a user signs up to the application.

Further reading

You can check out the following links for more information about the topics that were covered in this chapter:

- *What is Azure Active Directory B2C?*: `https://docs.microsoft.com/en-us/azure/active-directory-b2c/overview`

- *Clean up resources and delete the tenant*: `https://docs.microsoft.com/en-us/azure/active-directory-b2c/tutorial-delete-tenant`

- *Billing model for Azure Active Directory B2C*: `https://docs.microsoft.com/en-us/azure/active-directory-b2c/billing`

8

Advanced Features of Azure AD B2C

In the previous chapter, we covered the basics and built-in functionalities of Azure AD B2C. We created an Azure AD B2C tenant and added a user to it. Then, we covered how to create user flows in the Azure AD B2C tenant using the Azure portal. And finally, we used a sample application to connect to the Azure AD tenant using the SDKs that Microsoft provides, and signed in to Azure AD B2C.

In this chapter, we are going to build upon the previous chapter. We are going to look into identity providers in Azure AD B2C, and how you can configure them and add them to your user flows. We will use the sample application from the previous chapter to test this. Next, we are going to cover how you can change the UI of the default Azure AD B2C authentication experience so that it can be fully integrated into your application and looks like the branding of your custom applications. We are also going to look into what Microsoft Graph offers in conjunction with Azure AD B2C, and cover configuring custom domain names for Azure AD B2C.

The following topics will be covered in this chapter:

- Identity providers in Azure AD B2C
- Customizing the UI
- Localization and language customization

- Azure AD B2C and Microsoft Graph
- Custom domains for Azure AD B2C

Technical requirements

To follow this chapter, you need to have an active Azure subscription and to have completed all the demonstrations in *Chapter 7, Introducing Azure Active Directory B2C*.

Identity providers in Azure AD B2C

Azure AD B2C supports adding additional identity providers. Customers of your application can use these identity providers to sign in to your application. For instance, you can add social media identity providers to your application, and let users sign in with the credentials that belong to the social media account. Azure AD B2C supports several external identity providers, such as Apple, Amazon, Facebook, Google, GitHub, and LinkedIn.

> **Note**
>
> For a detailed overview of all the identity providers that are supported in Azure AD B2C, you can refer to the following article: `https://docs.microsoft.com/en-us/azure/active-directory-b2c/add-identity-provider#select-an-identity-provider`.

By adding external identity providers, you can give your customers the flexibility to choose how to sign in to your application. They can choose to use their social accounts, or maybe their Microsoft account, without having to create a new account only for your application. Once they have selected the identity provider they want to use, they are redirected to the website of the provider to complete the sign-in process. After successfully signing into the external provider's website, they are redirected to the Azure AD B2C authentication embedded in your custom website or application.

In the next demonstration, we are going to configure a LinkedIn identity provider.

Configuring the identity provider in Azure AD B2C

In this demonstration, we are going to configure a LinkedIn identity provider inside the Azure AD B2C portal and add it to the user flow that we created in the previous chapter. To do this, take the following steps:

1. Open a web browser and navigate to `https://portal.azure.com`.

2. In the top-right menu, select **Directories + subscriptions**, and make sure that the Azure AD B2C tenant we created in the previous chapter is selected.

3. Then, in the top search bar, search for **Azure AD B2C** and select it.

4. In the left menu, under **Manage**, select **Identity providers**. Then, in the list of supported identity providers, click on **LinkedIn**:

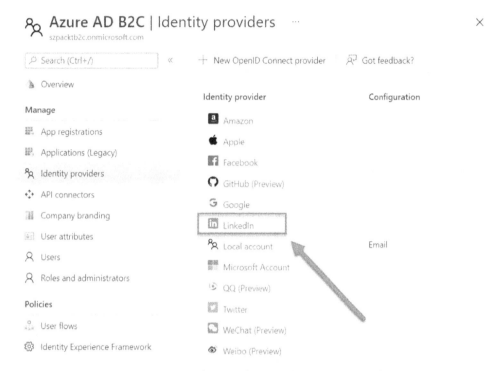

Figure 8.1 – Configuring the LinkedIn identity provider

A new page will open where you can configure the LinkedIn identity provider. Here, you need to specify the name, client ID, and client secret. The client ID and client secret need to be configured on the LinkedIn Developer website. Let's configure this first:

1. Open a new browser window and navigate to the LinkedIn Developer website: `https://developer.linkedin.com/`.

2. In the top menu, select **My apps**. Sign in with your LinkedIn credentials and click **Create app**.

3. Specify the following values to create the app:

    - **App name**: PacktB2CApp.

    - **LinkedIn Page**: Specify a company page here. If you don't have one, you can create a new one here as well.

    - **App logo**: Upload a logo here.

    - **Legal agreement**: Check the box here:

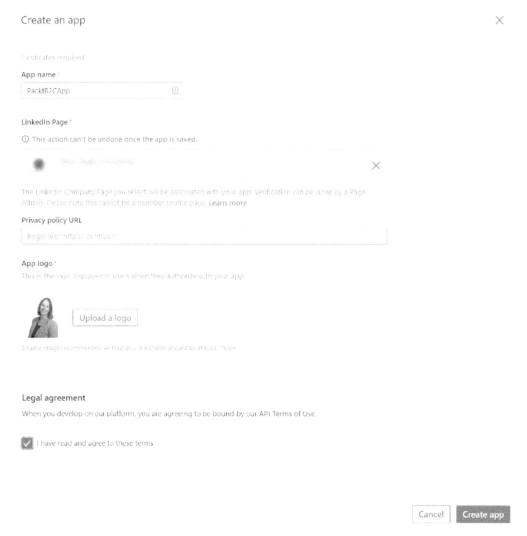

Figure 8.2 – Creating an app on the LinkedIn Developer website

4. Click **Create app**.

5. After creation, in the top menu, click **Auth**.

6. Here, you can copy the client ID and client secret. Copy them both and leave the LinkedIn window open.

7. Switch back to the Azure AD B2C tenant window where the configuration is still open. Give the identity provider a new name and paste both the client ID and client secret in the configuration:

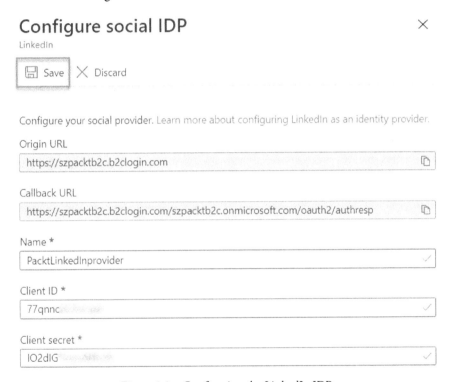

Figure 8.3 – Configuring the LinkedIn IDP

8. Copy the callback URL (we need to specify this URL in the LinkedIn app settings), and click the **Save** button.

9. Open the window again with the LinkedIn app settings, select the pencil next to **Authorized redirect URLs for your app**, select **+ Add redirect URL**, and paste in the callback URL that we copied in the previous step:

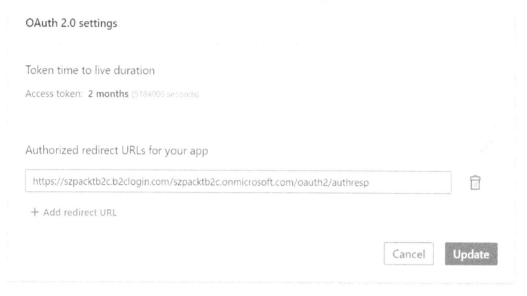

OAuth 2.0 settings

Token time to live duration

Access token: **2 months** (5184000 seconds)

Authorized redirect URLs for your app

https://szpacktb2c.b2clogin.com/szpacktb2c.onmicrosoft.com/oauth2/authresp

+ Add redirect URL

Cancel   **Update**

Figure 8.4 – Providing the redirect URL

10. Click **Update**.

11. Now, we need to approve the LinkedIn app for scopes related to signing in. Click **Products** in the top menu bar, select **Sign In with LinkedIn**, agree with the terms, and click **Add product**.

We have now configured the LinkedIn identity provider. In the next step, we are going to add the identity provider to the user flow and test it.

Adding the LinkedIn identity provider to the user flow

Configured identity providers can be added to different user flows. This makes them very flexible; you can easily add and remove them from the user flows in the Azure AD B2C tenant using the Azure portal.

We are going to add this identity provider to the **B2C_1_packtsignupsignin** user flow that we created in the previous chapter:

1. In the Azure AD tenant in the Azure portal, under **Policies**, select **User flows**. Then, in the overview, click on the **B2C_1_packtsignupsignin** flow. The settings for this flow will be displayed.

2. In the left menu, select **Identity providers**. Here, you will see the LinkedIn IDP displayed. Select it:

▷ Run user flow   💾 Save   ✕ Discard   ⊗ Manage identity providers   ⧉ Got feedback?

Identity providers are the different types of accounts your users can use to sign up or sign in to your application. You need to select at least one for a valid user flow. Learn more about identity providers.

Local accounts

◉ Email signup

◯ None

Social identity providers

Identity Provider	Name
☑ 🔗 LinkedIn	PacktLinkedInprovider

Figure 8.5 – Adding the IDP to the user flow

3. Click **Save** in the top menu.

4. We have now added the LinkedIn identity provider to the user flow. The last step is to test and see whether we can sign in using our LinkedIn account.

5. In the top menu, select **Run user flow**.

6. Make sure **PacktB2CApp** is selected and that `https://jwt.ms/` is selected under **Reply URL**:

Figure 8.6 – Testing user flow

7. Click on **Run user flow**.

8. This will load the authentication experience of Azure AD B2C, and you will see that the LinkedIn identity provider is added to it:

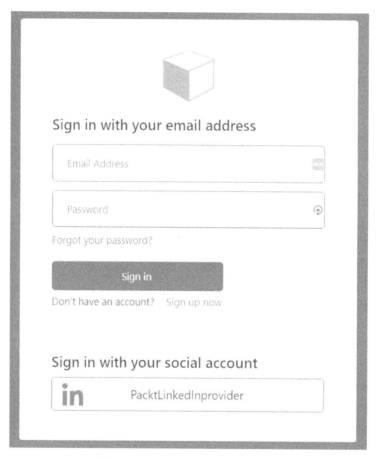

Figure 8.7 – IDP on the sign-in page

9. Click on the IDP button, and you will be redirected to the LinkedIn sign-in page. Log in with your credentials and give consent. You will be sent back to Azure AD B2C, where you need to specify the additional profile information that is configured in the user flow:

Figure 8.8 – Providing additional profile information

It is good to note here that Azure AD B2C uses the identity provider to sign in the user. But, what actually happens is that Azure AD B2C also creates a new user in the tenant (as a local account). It is storing the profile information here and links it to the identity provider.

10. Click **Continue**.

11. After that, you will be redirected again to the `https://jwt.ms/` website, which displays the access token and the claims. It now has an extra claim called `idp` with a `linkedin.com` value:

```
Decoded Token    Claims

{
  "typ": "JWT",
  "alg": "RS256",
  "kid": "X5eXk4xyojNFum1kl2Ytv8dlNP4-c57dO6QGTVBwaNk"
}.{
  "exp": 1640788990,
  "nbf": 1640785390,
  "ver": "1.0",
  "iss": "https://szpacktb2c.b2clogin.com/d3880203-622e-4229-9dd0-93eaecff6ed9/v2.0/",
  "sub": "e50ce010-c2c3-45c9-8856-0298a29559bf",
  "aud": "19bc47f2-25d8-44f3-80ff-2ffb7cc67d71",
  "nonce": "defaultNonce",
  "iat": 1640785390,
  "auth_time": 1640785390,
  "idp": "linkedin.com",
  "name": "Sjoukje Zaal",
  "country": "Netherlands",
  "postalCode": "HG 9832",
  "streetAddress": "PacktRoad 1",
  "tfp": "B2C_1_packtsignupsignin"
}.[Signature]
```

Figure 8.9 – IDP on the sign-in page

We have now configured the LinkedIn identity provider, added it to a user flow, and tested it successfully in the Azure AD B2C tenant. In the next section, we are going to cover how you can customize the UI of the Azure AD authentication experience.

Customizing the UI

To create a seamless user experience in your custom websites or applications, you may want to customize the UI of the authentication experiences in Azure AD B2C. In the previous demonstrations, we used the default UI provided by Azure AD B2C; you can customize this by creating your own HTML and CSS pages and referring to them from the user flows that you have configured for your applications.

You can create these pages using your own branding. These pages can be built using static HTML files, but you can also use .NET, PHP, or Node.js files. The only requirement for Azure AD B2C is that it contains a `div` element, with `id` set to `api`. Azure AD B2C needs that `div` element to know where it needs to inject the code for the user flows.

The following code is an example of a very basic HTML file with the `div` element added to it:

```
<!DOCTYPE html>
<html>
<head>
    <title>My website</title>
</head>
<body>
    <div id="api"></div>
</body>
</html>
```

> **Note**
>
> Instead of creating these pages from scratch, Microsoft provides a set of default pages that you can customize. There are multiple types of pages that you can download: `exception.html`, `selfasserted.html`, `multifactor-1.0.0.html`, `updateprofile.html`, and `unified.html`. You can download them here: `https://docs.microsoft.com/en-us/azure/active-directory-b2c/customize-ui-with-html?pivots=b2c-user-flow#customize-the-default-azure-ad-b2c-pages`.

Once you have created these files, you can host the UI content on any publicly available HTTPS endpoint. The only requirement is that it needs to support **cross-origin resource sharing** (**CORS**). For instance, you can upload them to Azure Blob storage, CDNs, Azure App Service, AWS S3, or file-sharing systems.

When the UI content is hosted on a publicly available HTTPS endpoint, you can configure this in the user flow settings. For this, you need to take the following steps:

1. From the **B2C_1_packtsignupsignin** user flow overview page, in the left menu, under **Customize**, click on **Page layouts**.

2. Under **Unified sign up or sign in page | Use custom page content**, select **Yes**.

3. Set **Custom page URI** to where the HTML page can be accessed. Ensure that CORS is configured for this endpoint:

Figure 8.10 – Customizing the UI

4. Click **Save** in the top menu.

Now that we have covered how you can customize the UI of your user experiences, we are going to cover how you can localize your custom pages in Azure AD B2C in the next section.

Localization and language customization

You can use the localization and language customization features to select which languages your user flow is available in to suit your applications and customers' needs. Microsoft provides 36 languages in Azure AD B2C, and if your required language isn't available, you can also provide your own translations for any language.

Once you have selected the languages that you want to make available to the user flow, you can provide a `ui_locales` query string parameter from your application. When you make a request to Azure AD B2C that includes this query string parameter, your page will be translated to the locale you have provided in the query string.

> **Note**
>
> For more information on this and how to set up the application code, you can refer to the following article: `https://docs.microsoft.com/en-us/azure/active-directory-b2c/language-customization?pivots=b2c-user-flow`.

To enable localization and language customization for your user flows, take the following steps:

1. You can enable language customization for the user flows in the Azure AD B2C tenant. From the user flow settings, under **Customize**, you can select **Languages**:

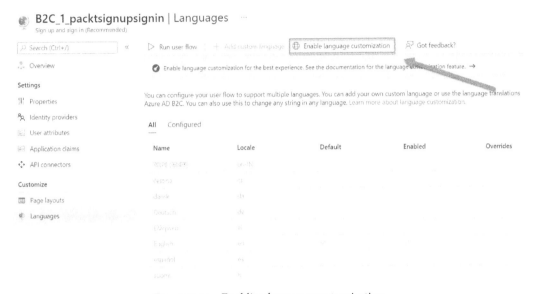

Figure 8.11 – Enabling language customization

2. Here, you can enable it by selecting **Enable language customization** from the top menu and selecting the languages you want to make available for this user flow. If you want to upload your own translations, you can do that here as well.

Now that we have briefly covered localization and language customization in Azure AD B2C, we will move on to Azure AD B2C and Microsoft Graph.

Azure AD B2C and Microsoft Graph

Microsoft Graph provides functionality to manage your Azure AD B2C resources. It provides several operations that you can use to create and manage the Azure B2C tenant, create users, and manage identity providers, user flows, and custom policies.

Before you can use the Microsoft Graph API to access the Azure AD B2C tenant, you first need to register an application inside Azure AD B2C that grants the permissions.

> **Note**
>
> Registering the application to grant permissions to Microsoft Graph is beyond the scope of this book. For more information on how to register this, you can refer to the following: `https://docs.microsoft.com/en-us/azure/active-directory-b2c/microsoft-graph-get-started?tabs=app-reg-ga#register-management-application`.

To interact with your Azure B2C tenant from the Microsoft Graph API, there is support for the following:

- **User management**: You can retrieve a list of users, create a user, update, and delete a user.

- **Applications**: You can get a list of registered applications in Azure AD B2C, and create, update, and delete applications. You can also create a `servicePrincipal` and an `oauth2Permission` grant.

- **Identity providers**: There is support to list identity providers, and create, get, update, and delete identity providers.

- **User flows**: From Microsoft Graph, you can list, get, create, and delete user flows in Azure AD B2C.

- **Custom policies**: There is also support for managing your custom policies in Azure AD B2C (custom policies are covered in more detail in the next chapter). You can also list all custom policies, create a custom policy, read properties from the custom policies, and update and delete them as well.

- **Audit logs**: Azure AD B2C also has login and monitoring capabilities that can be listed using the Microsoft Graph API.

- **Conditional Access**: You can get a list of Conditional Access policies, retrieve properties and relationships, and create, update, and delete Conditional Access policies.

- **Phone number management (currently in beta)**: Phone numbers can be added for MFA purposes. You can add, list, get, update, and delete user phone numbers using the Microsoft Graph API.

- **Self-service password reset email address (currently in beta)**: This email address can be used to reset the password of the user. The Microsoft Graph API has support for adding, listing, getting, updating, and deleting email addresses.

- **Software OATH token authentication method (currently in beta)**: An OATH token is a software-based number generator that is used in the Microsoft Authenticator app for MFA. It generates a number that uses the OATH **time-based one-time password (TOTP)** standard.

> **Note**
>
> For more detailed information about all the operations of Microsoft Graph for Azure AD B2C, you can refer to the following website: `https://docs.microsoft.com/en-us/azure/active-directory-b2c/microsoft-graph-operations`. If you want to test these operations, you can use the Graph Explorer that we also used for our demonstration in *Chapter 6*, *Building Secure Services Using the Microsoft Graph API*.

Now that we have an overview of what operations are supported by the Microsoft Graph API, we will cover custom domains in Azure AD B2C next.

Custom domains for Azure AD B2C

To provide a more seamless user experience, you can configure custom domains for Azure AD B2C using Azure Front Door. Azure Front Door is a separate service in Azure that offers layer 7 load-balancing capabilities for your applications. It provides a global and scalable entry point that uses the Microsoft global edge network and improves global connectivity and scalability for your applications and websites.

The Azure AD B2C content is rendered behind Azure Front Door, and then Azure Front Door has a configuration option to deliver the content to your application's URL via the custom domain.

The following diagram gives an overview of the Azure Front Door integration with Azure AD B2C:

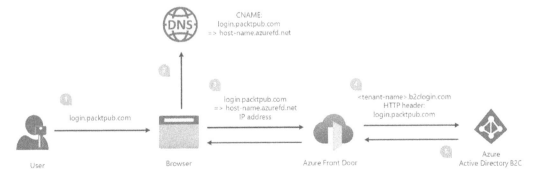

Figure 8.12 – Custom domain in Azure B2C using Azure Front Door

The following is the breakdown of the steps mentioned:

1. From your custom application or website, the user clicks the sign-in button, which will trigger the user flow and then redirects the user to the Azure AD B2C sign-in page.

2. The custom domain name will then be resolved by the web browser using DNS. There will be a CNAME record with a custom domain added that will redirect the traffic to the Azure Front Door IP address (to the default frontend host). For example, this can be `packt-frontend.azurefd.net`.

3. The traffic will then be routed from the original URL, which is `login.packtpub.com`, to the Front Door default frontend host, which is `packt-frontend.azurefd.net`.

4. Azure Front Door will then revoke Azure AD B2C content using the Azure AD B2C `<tenant-name>.b2clogin.com` default domain. The request sent to this endpoint will include the original custom domain name (`login.packtpub.com`).

5. Azure AD B2C will then respond to this request by displaying the original domain name (`login.packtpub.com`) and relevant content for the request.

Consider the following when you decide to use custom domain names for Azure AD B2C using Azure Front Door:

- You can set up multiple custom domains for Azure AD B2C, but there is a limit to the number of additional custom domains that can be used in conjunction with Azure AD B2C. For more information about these limits, you can refer to the *Azure AD service limits and restrictions* article at `https://docs.microsoft.com/en-us/azure/active-directory/enterprise-users/directory-service-limits-restrictions`, and also the *Azure subscription and service limits, quotas, and constraints for Azure Front Door* article at `https://docs.microsoft.com/en-us/azure/azure-resource-manager/management/azure-subscription-service-limits#azure-front-door-service-limits`.

- Azure Front Door is a separate service, so you should be aware that this will result in additional costs.

- Even when a custom domain name is configured, the default domain name for Azure AD B2C can be accessed. If you want to disable access to this, you need to create a custom policy to block access. You can refer to this article for more information on how to block this: `https://docs.microsoft.com/en-us/azure/active-directory-b2c/custom-domain?pivots=b2c-user-flow#block-access-to-the-default-domain-name`.

- If you have multiple applications and websites that use Azure AD B2C for authentication, it is recommended to migrate them all to the custom domain. The Azure AD B2C session is stored by the browser under the domain name currently being used.

In this last section of this chapter, we have covered how you can configure custom domains for Azure AD B2C using Azure Front Door. This concludes this chapter.

Summary

In this chapter, we have focused on the more advanced features of Azure AD B2C. We have covered how you can configure identity providers in Azure AD B2C, and we configured a LinkedIn identity provider as an example. Then, we looked at how you can customize the UI to create a seamless user experience. We touched on how you can add localization and language customization in Azure AD B2C for supporting multi-lingual websites and applications. We also focused on the integration of Azure AD B2C in Microsoft Graph, and how you can add custom domains using Azure Front Door for Azure AD B2C.

In the next and last chapter of this book, we will focus on custom policies in Azure AD B2C. These custom policies are created inside the Identity Experience Framework, which we are also going to cover.

Further reading

You can check out the following links for more information about the topics that were covered in this chapter:

- *Set up sign-up and sign-in with a LinkedIn account using Azure Active Directory B2C*: https://docs.microsoft.com/en-us/azure/active-directory-b2c/identity-provider-linkedin?pivots=b2c-user-flow

- *Customize the user interface with HTML templates in Azure Active Directory B2C*: https://docs.microsoft.com/en-us/azure/active-directory-b2c/customize-ui-with-html?pivots=b2c-user-flow#customize-the-default-azure-ad-b2c-pages

- *Supported languages*: https://docs.microsoft.com/en-us/azure/active-directory-b2c/language-customization?pivots=b2c-user-flow#supported-languages

- *Manage Azure AD B2C with Microsoft Graph*: `https://docs.microsoft.com/en-us/azure/active-directory-b2c/microsoft-graph-operations`

- *Enable custom domains for Azure Active Directory B2C*: `https://docs.microsoft.com/en-us/azure/active-directory-b2c/custom-domain?pivots=b2c-user-flow`.

9
Azure AD B2C Custom Policies

In the previous chapter, we covered some more of the advanced features of Azure AD B2C. We looked at how you can configure identity providers in Azure AD B2C. We configured a LinkedIn identity provider inside Azure AD B2C and added it to the user flow we created in *Chapter 7, Introducing Azure Active Directory B2C*. Next, we covered how you can customize the UI and localization and looked at the integration of Azure AD B2C in Microsoft Graph.

In this last chapter, we are going to dive into custom policies. This is a topic on its own, and that's why I dedicated a whole chapter to it. We will look into custom policies and what they can bring to your custom applications. We are going to cover the Identity Experience Framework briefly, and you will learn the connection between custom policies and the Identity Experience Framework. And finally, we will create our own custom policy that connects to an Azure function and stores user profile information inside Azure Table storage.

The following topics will be covered in this chapter:

- Understanding custom policies

- Introducing the Identity Experience Framework

- Creating a custom policy

Technical requirements

To follow this chapter, you need to have an active Azure subscription to create an Azure AD B2C tenant. You also need to have the latest version of Visual Studio or Visual Studio Code installed:

- Visual Studio Code: `https://code.visualstudio.com/`

- Visual Studio: `https://visualstudio.microsoft.com/`

I'm going to use Visual Studio Code for the examples in this chapter, but of course, you can use Visual Studio as well.

You can download the source code of this chapter here: `https://github.com/PacktPublishing/Azure-Active-Directory-for-Developers/tree/main/Chapter%209/Custom%20Policy`.

Understanding custom policies

Custom policies in Azure AD B2C are basically configuration files that can be created to define the Azure AD tenant user experience. In the previous chapter, we covered user flows in Azure AD B2C. They are predefined and are offered as templates that you can configure to cover the most common identity scenarios. However, in some cases, these user flows are not sufficient, and you need to create your own user experiences. In these cases, you can build custom policies. These policies can be configured by developers and then uploaded to the Azure AD B2C tenant. Scenarios in which you need to create custom policies can be when you need to collect user input and store it in a separate database, such as a CRM system, or a custom profile database. Or, in cases when you need to use a custom **multi-factor authentication** (**MFA**) product, you can also integrate this into a custom policy.

Custom policies are defined by creating a set of XML configuration files that refer to each other. The claims schema, claims transformations, content definitions, claims providers, technical profiles, user journey orchestration steps, and other aspects of the identity experience are defined inside these XML files using different XML elements.

Microsoft offers an Azure AD custom policy starter pack, which provides a set of pre-built policies that you can use for different scenarios. Using this starter pack, developers don't have to build the XML files from scratch but can pick the example that is most similar to the sign-in scenario that is required for their custom application or website, and then make changes accordingly. The following technical profiles and user journeys are provided in the starter pack:

- `LocalAccounts`: This sample can be used in scenarios where only local accounts are used in Azure AD B2C.

- `SocialAccounts`: This sample can be used in scenarios where only social accounts are used in conjunction with Azure AD B2C.

- `SocialAndLocalAccounts`: This combines both local and social accounts.

- `SocialAndLocalAccountsWithMFA`: This adds MFA support to the previous example.

> **Note**
> You can download the starter pack from the Microsoft documentation site: `https://docs.microsoft.com/en-us/azure/active-directory-b2c/tutorial-create-user-flows?pivots=b2c-custom-policy#get-the-starter-pack`.

Each custom policy in the starter pack includes the following XML files:

- **Base file**: This file contains most definitions. It is recommended to make as few changes as possible to this file, to help with troubleshooting when errors occur and for maintenance purposes of the policy.

- **Localization file**: This file stores the localization strings. This policy is derived from the base file and is used to support different languages when this is required for the scenario.

- **Extensions file**: This file is derived from the localization file and stores unique configuration changes for your Azure AD B2C tenant. In this file, you can add new functionality that overrides the existing functionality. So, instead of making changes to the base file, you use this file to add new functionality, such as federating with new identity providers.

- **Relying Party file**: This file is derived from the extensions file and is the single task-focused file that is called directly from the application. This application can be your custom web, desktop, or mobile application. Each task, such as a sign-up, sign-in, and profile edit task, requires having its own *Relying Party* file.

> **Note**
>
> For more detailed information about all the elements inside the custom policy files, you can refer to the following article: `https://docs.microsoft.com/en-us/azure/active-directory-b2c/custom-policy-overview`.

When you start developing custom policies, you can run into exceptions or errors while you are running the custom user journeys that you create with custom policies. Take the following recommendations into account when you start creating custom policies:

- Debugging and troubleshooting can be done by using Application Insights. You can integrate Application Insights with Azure AD B2C. For more information, refer to the following website: `https://docs.microsoft.com/en-us/azure/active-directory-b2c/troubleshoot-with-application-insights?pivots=b2c-user-flow`.

- Download the Azure AD B2C extension for Visual Studio Code. This can help you access the logs and visualize them. You can download the extension here: `https://marketplace.visualstudio.com/items?itemName=AzureADB2CTools.aadb2c`.

- XML can be difficult to troubleshoot. Custom policies are completely built using XML files. Use XML schema validation to ensure that the XML is properly formatted.

Microsoft recommends using the built-in user flows that Azure B2C provides, and only creating custom policies if there is no other option available. Custom policies are difficult to build, maintain, and debug. Besides custom policies, there is another option that developers can use to add additional functionalities to the user flows. You can use API connectors to customize and extend user flows with external identity data sources.

> **Note**
>
> For more information about using API connectors in Azure AD B2C, you can refer to the following: `https://docs.microsoft.com/en-us/azure/active-directory-b2c/api-connectors-overview?pivots=b2c-user-flow`.

In the next section, we are going to introduce the Identity Experience Framework, which is basically the engine for custom development in Azure AD B2C.

Introducing the Identity Experience Framework

The Identity Experience Framework is an identity engine and orchestration platform that is used internally for Azure services such as Azure AD B2C. Using this framework, developers can create their own user journeys and integrate multiple identity providers and other data sources. These user journeys are created in the form of custom policies.

Features that are included in the Identity Experience Framework are as follows:

- Creating and uploading custom policies, which include custom user journeys. You can define `if-then` branching inside these custom policies, and map and transform claims to be used for your authorization strategy inside your custom applications (making decisions based on these claims).

- Interact with REST API services, such as CRM systems, external databases, email providers, and external authorization systems.

- Using custom policies, you can federate with SAML 2.0 providers, such as ADFS and Salesforce. This is not possible using out-of-the-box user flows. If you have this requirement for your application, creating a custom policy is the only option.

To stay up to date with future releases of the Identity Experience Framework, you can refer to the following article: `https://docs.microsoft.com/en-us/azure/active-directory-b2c/custom-policy-developer-notes`.

In the next section, we are going to create our own custom policy and upload it to the Identity Experience Framework in our Azure AD B2C tenant.

Creating a custom policy

In this demonstration, we are going to create a custom policy to store user information inside Azure Blob storage during the sign-up experience. Users will be asked to check a box that asks them whether they want to retrieve marketing information. If they check this box, the user details, such as the name and the email address, will be stored inside Azure Table storage. The custom policy will call an Azure function, which will then store the user details in the table.

The scenario will look like the following figure:

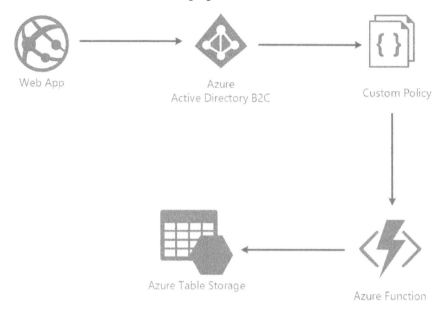

Figure 9.1 – Custom policy scenario figure

Let's start with the first step of this demonstration and prepare the Azure AD B2C tenant by registering the signing and encryption key in the Identity Experience Framework.

Creating the signing and encryption key

Before we can upload the custom policy, we first need to create a signing and encryption key inside the Identity Experience Framework in Azure AD B2C:

1. Open a web browser and navigate to `https://portal.azure.com`.

2. Navigate to the Azure AD B2C tenant. In the overview page of **Azure AD B2C**, in the left menu, under **Policies**, click **Identity Experience Framework**.

3. Then, under **Manage**, select **Policy keys**.

4. Click **+ Add** in the top menu. First, we are going to create the signing key:

    - **Options**: Generate
    - **Name**: TokenSigningKeyContainer (the prefix B2C_1A_ will be added automatically)
    - **Key type**: RSA
    - **Key usage**: Signature

Figure 9.2 – Creating a signing key

5. Click **Create**.

6. To create the encryption key, use these details:

    - **Options**: Generate
    - **Name**: TokenEncryptionKeyContainer (the prefix B2C_1A_ will be added automatically)
    - **Key type**: Secret

- **Key usage**: Encryption

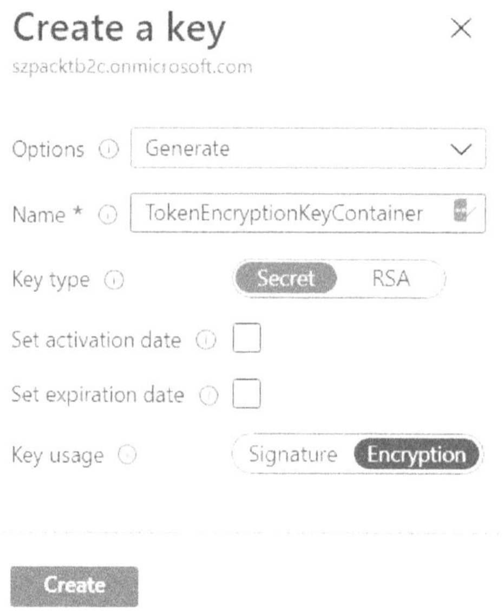

Figure 9.3 – Creating an encryption key

7.   Click **Create**.

Now that both the signing and encryption keys are created, we can register the Identity Experience Framework applications.

Registering the Identity Experience Framework applications

In this demonstration, we are going to create a custom policy that is built for the sign-up and sign-in users with local accounts experience. Therefore, we need to register two applications inside the Identity Experience Framework.

We need to register a web API, called `IdentityExperienceFramework`, and we need to register a native app with delegated permissions to the `IdentityExperienceFramework` app called `ProxyIdentityExperienceFramework`. Users can sign up with an email address and their password to access the tenant-registered applications, which will create a local account in this scenario. This account is then stored inside the Azure AD B2C tenant.

These two app registrations only need to be registered once in your tenant. All future custom policies can then use these two registered applications.

To register the applications, we need to take the following steps:

1. On the **Identity Experience Framework** overview page, in the left menu, select **App Registrations**. Then, in the top menu, click on **+ New registration**.

2. Provide the following values:

   - **Name**: IdentityExperienceFramework.

   - **Supported account types**: Accounts in any identity provider or organizational directory (for authenticating users with user flows).

   - **Redirect URI**: Select **Web** and then provide the following: https://<tenantname>.b2clogin.com/<tenant-name>. onmicrosoft.com (replace <tenant-name> with your actual tenant name).

   - **Permissions**: Ensure **Grant admin consent to openid and offline_access permissions** is selected:

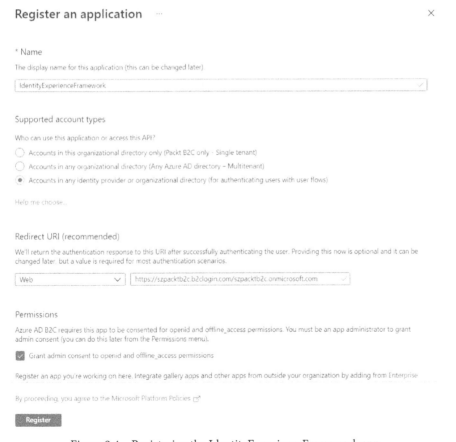

Figure 9.4 – Registering the IdentityExperienceFramework app

3. Click **Register**.

4. Next, we need to expose the API by adding a scope to it. In the left menu, under **Manage**, click **Expose an API**.

5. Select **Add a scope** in the top menu, and then keep the default application ID URI and click **Save and continue**:

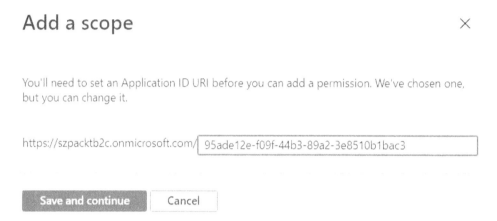

Figure 9.5 – Setting the application ID URI

6. To create the scope, add the following values:

*   **Scope name**: user_impersonation

*   **Admin consent display name**: Access IdentityExperienceFramework

*   **Admin consent description**: Allow the application to access IdentityExperienceFramework on behalf of the signed-in user.

- **State: Enabled**

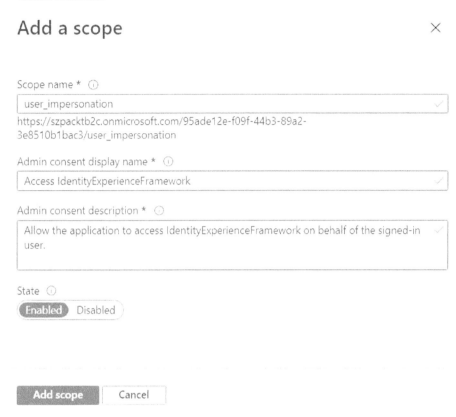

Figure 9.6 – Adding a scope

7. Click **Add scope**.

8. Next, we are going to register the `ProxyIdentityExperienceFramework` application. In the **App registrations overview** blade, select **+ New registration** again.

9.   Provide the following values:

- **Name**: `ProxyIdentityExperienceFramework`.

- **Supported account types**: **Accounts in this organizational directory only**.

- **Redirect URI**: Select **Public client/native (mobile and desktop)** and provide the following URI: `myapp://auth`.

- **Permissions**: Ensure **Grant admin consent to openid and offline_access permissions** is selected:

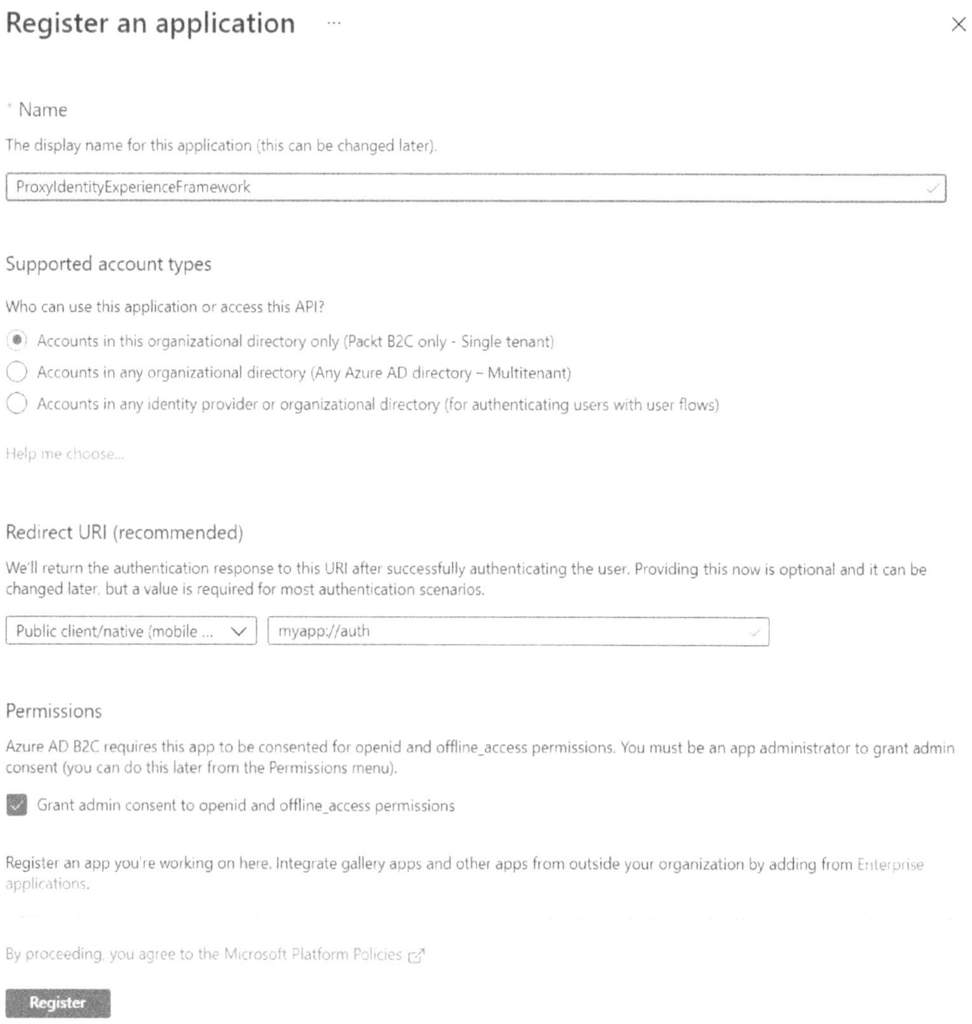

Register an application   ···   ×

* Name

The display name for this application (this can be changed later).

ProxyIdentityExperienceFramework   ✓

Supported account types

Who can use this application or access this API?

◉ Accounts in this organizational directory only (Packt B2C only - Single tenant)

◯ Accounts in any organizational directory (Any Azure AD directory – Multitenant)

◯ Accounts in any identity provider or organizational directory (for authenticating users with user flows)

Help me choose...

Redirect URI (recommended)

We'll return the authentication response to this URI after successfully authenticating the user. Providing this now is optional and it can be changed later, but a value is required for most authentication scenarios.

| Public client/native (mobile ... ∨ | myapp://auth   ✓ |

Permissions

Azure AD B2C requires this app to be consented for openid and offline_access permissions. You must be an app administrator to grant admin consent (you can do this later from the Permissions menu).

☑ Grant admin consent to openid and offline_access permissions

Register an app you're working on here. Integrate gallery apps and other apps from outside your organization by adding from Enterprise applications.

By proceeding, you agree to the Microsoft Platform Policies ☐

Register

Figure 9.7 – Registering the ProxyIdentityExperienceFramework app

10. Click **Register**.

11. After the registration is completed, copy the application (client) ID to Notepad.

12. Now, we need to configure the application that is treated as a public client. In the left menu, under **Manage**, select **Authentication**.

13. Under **Advanced settings | Allow public client flows**, set **Enable the following mobile and desktop flows** to **Yes**.

14. Click **Save** in the top menu bar.

15. We need to check whether this setting is also added to the application manifest. In the left menu, under **Manage**, select **Manifest**. Search for the `allowPublicClient` key and make sure that is it set to `true`:

```
🖫 Save  ✕ Discard   ⬆ Upload   ⬇ Download    ⚲ Got feedback?

The editor below allows you to update this application by directly modifying its JSON representation. For more details, see: Understanding the Azure Active Directory application manifest

 1   {
 2       "id": "89f1704b-145a-45be-8150-e0954b9455ba",
 3       "acceptMappedClaims": null,
 4       "accessTokenAcceptedVersion": null,
 5       "addIns": [],
 6       "allowPublicClient": true,
 7       "appId": "89110821-75dc-42fd-997d-17606aa01b4e",
 8       "appRoles": [],
 9       "oauth2AllowUrlPathMatching": false,
10       "createdDateTime": "2021-12-29T08:50:18Z",
11       "description": null,
12       "certification": null,
13       "disabledByMicrosoftStatus": null,
14       "groupMembershipClaims": null,
15       "identifierUris": [],
16       "informationalUrls": {
17           "termsOfService": null,
18           "support": null,
19           "privacy": null,
20           "marketing": null
```

Figure 9.8 – Application manifest

The last step is to grant permissions to the API scope that we created in the previous step:

1. In the left menu, under **Manage**, select **API permissions**.

2. Then, in the top menu, select **+ Add a permission**.

3. Select **My APIs**, then select **IdentityExperienceFramework**.

4.   Under **Permission**, select **user_impersonation**:

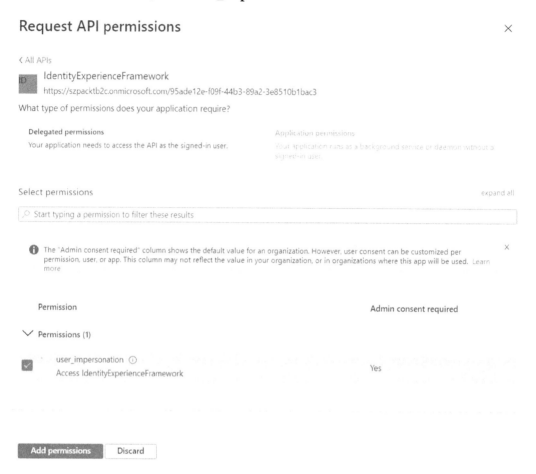

Figure 9.9 – Adding permissions

5.   Click **Add permissions**.

6.   Next, select **Grant admin consent for <tenant-name>**:

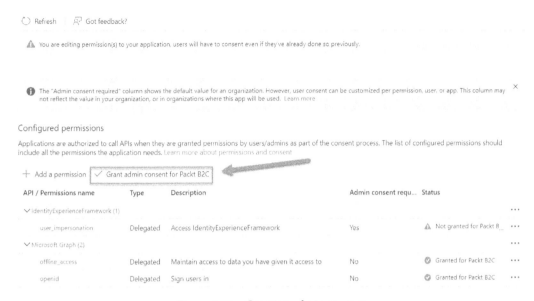

Figure 9.10 – Granting admin consent

7. Click **Yes**.

We have now finished registering the application registrations and setting the required scopes and permissions. In the next section, we are going to set up the table storage account in Azure, which we are going to use to store the user profile information.

Creating the Azure storage account

The next step is to create the Azure Table storage account where the user details will be stored. For this, take the following steps:

1. Open a web browser and navigate to `https://portal.azure.com/#home`.

2. Ensure that you have the right Azure AD tenant selected. The storage account cannot be created inside the Azure AD B2C tenant. In the top-right menu bar, select **Directories + subscriptions** and switch to an Azure AD tenant.

3. In the top search bar, search for `Storage accounts` and select it.

4. In the top menu, click **+ Create** to create a new storage account. Add the following values to create a new storage account:

   - **Subscription**: Select a subscription here.

   - **Resource group**: Select the **packtb2c-rg** group that we created earlier for the Azure AD B2C tenant.

- **Storage account name:** `packtb2cstorage`.

- **Region:** West US.

- **Performance:** Standard.

- **Redundancy:** Locally-redundant storage (LRS):

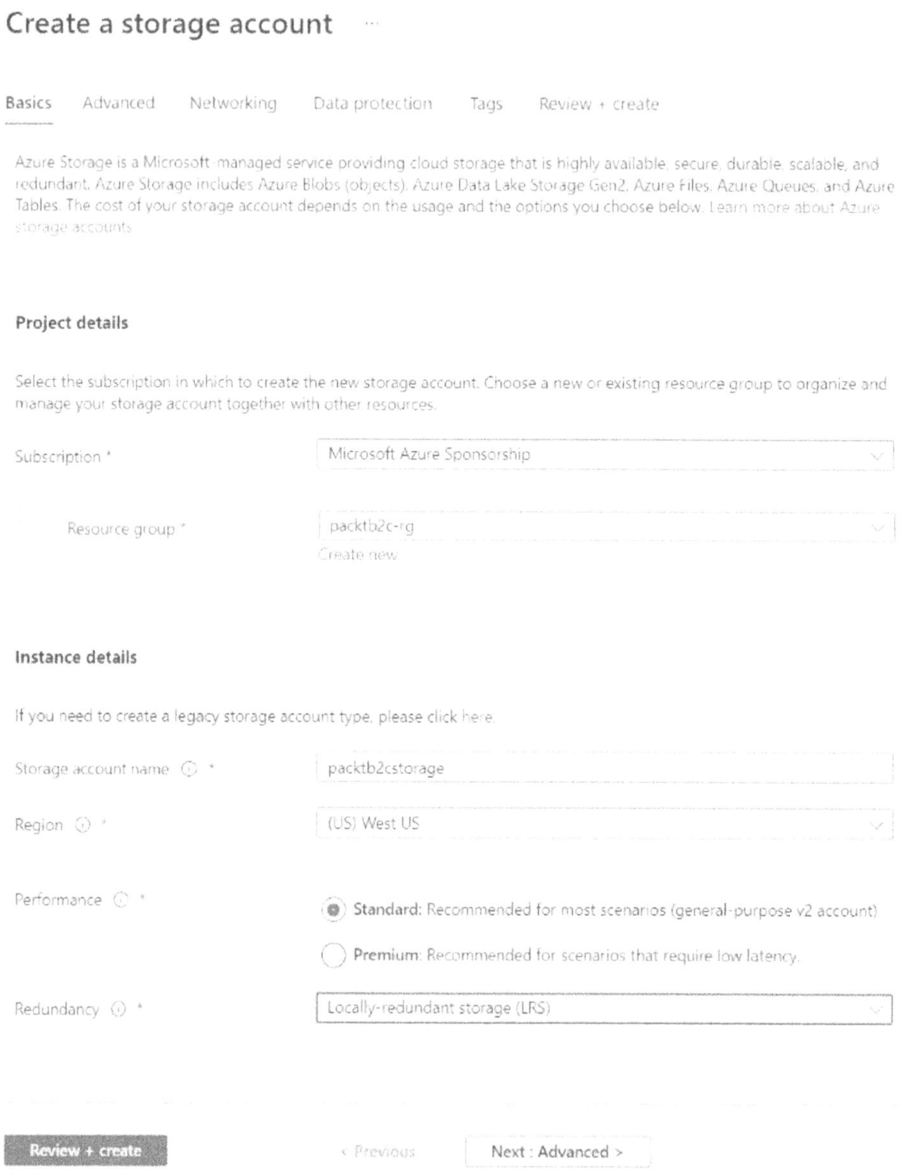

Figure 9.11 – Storage account settings

5. When the deployment is finished, click the link displayed on the deployment page, which lets you navigate to the new storage account. You can also navigate to the storage account from the search bar or the resources overview page.

6. In the left menu, under **Data storage**, select **Tables**. In the top menu, click **+ Create Table**. Provide `B2CMarketing` as the table name.

Now that we have created the storage account and a table, we can create the Azure function that is going to store the user details inside the table storage.

Creating the Azure function

In this part of the demonstration, we are going to create the Azure function. To do this, take the following steps:

1. Open a web browser and navigate to `https://portal.azure.com`.

2. In the top search bar, search for `Function App` and select it.

3. In the top menu, click **+ Create** to create a new function app. Add the following values:

   - **Subscription**: Select a subscription here.

   - **Resource Group**: Select the **packtb2c-rg** that we created earlier for the Azure AD B2C tenant.

   - **Function App name**: Provide a unique name here, I've used `PacktB2CMarketing`.

   - **Publish**: **Code**.

   - **Runtime stack**: .NET.

   - **Version**: **6**.

- **Region**: West US.

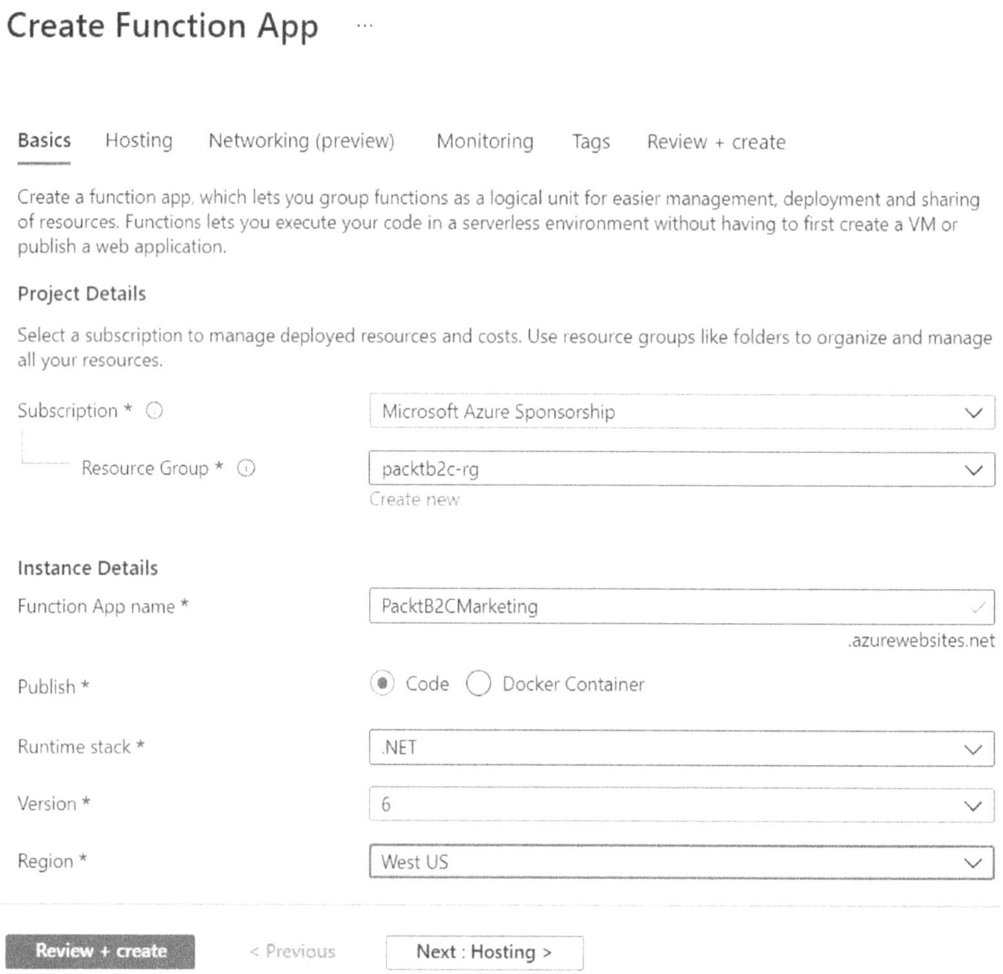

Figure 9.12 – Creating a function app

4.   Click **Review + create**. And next, click **Create**.

5.   The function app will be created. After the deployment completes, click the **Go to resource** button.

6. In the left menu, under **Functions**, select **Functions**. Click **+ Create** to create a new function. Make sure that **Develop in portal** is selected and select **HTTP trigger**. We are going to make an HTTP request from the custom policy. Name the function `AddUserToTableStorage` and keep the default authorization level, which is set to **Function**:

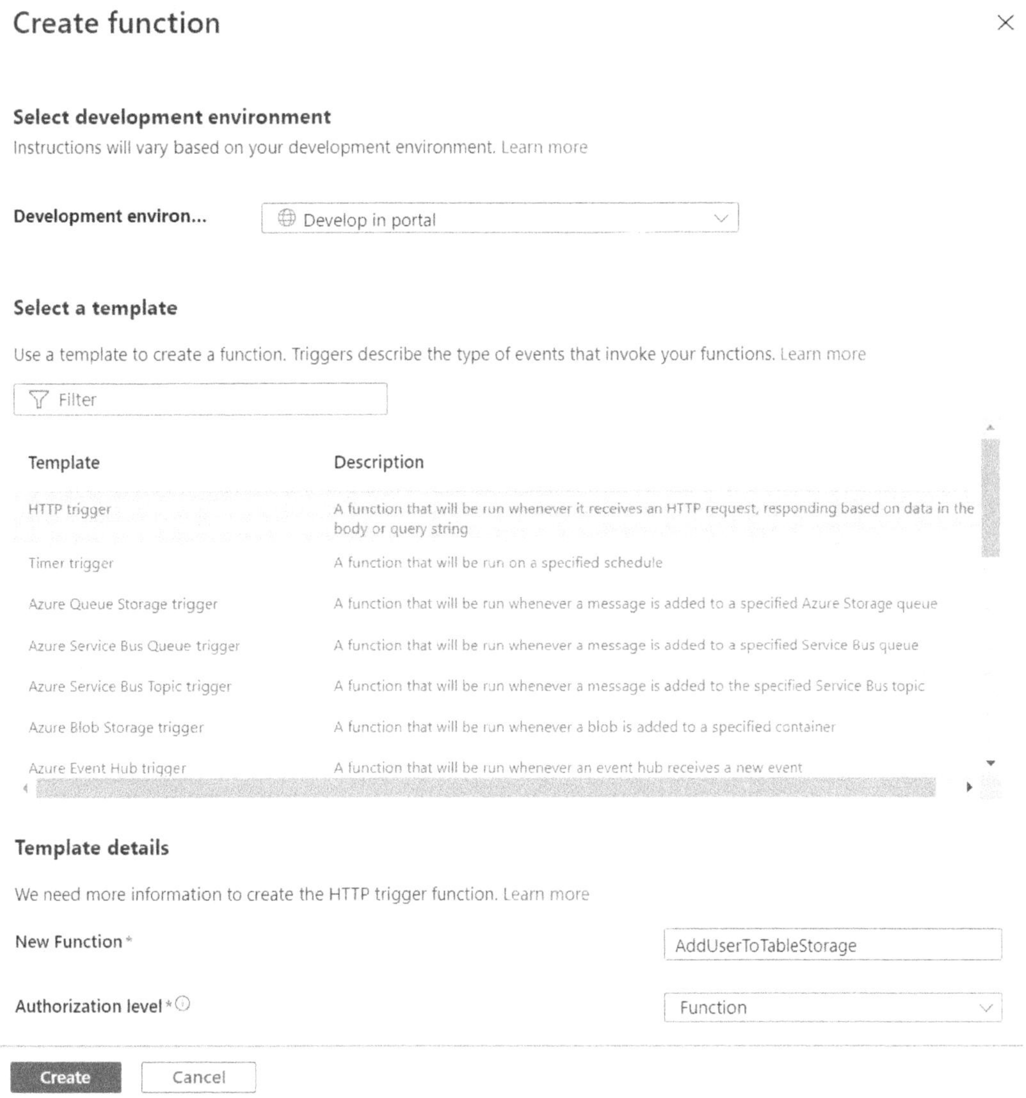

Create function   ✕

Select development environment

Instructions will vary based on your development environment. Learn more

Development environ... | ⊕ Develop in portal   ˅ |

Select a template

Use a template to create a function. Triggers describe the type of events that invoke your functions. Learn more

▽ Filter

Template	Description
HTTP trigger	A function that will be run whenever it receives an HTTP request, responding based on data in the body or query string
Timer trigger	A function that will be run on a specified schedule
Azure Queue Storage trigger	A function that will be run whenever a message is added to a specified Azure Storage queue
Azure Service Bus Queue trigger	A function that will be run whenever a message is added to a specified Service Bus queue
Azure Service Bus Topic trigger	A function that will be run whenever a message is added to the specified Service Bus topic
Azure Blob Storage trigger	A function that will be run whenever a blob is added to a specified container
Azure Event Hub trigger	A function that will be run whenever an event hub receives a new event

Template details

We need more information to create the HTTP trigger function. Learn more

New Function * | AddUserToTableStorage |

Authorization level * ⓘ | Function   ˅ |

[Create]   [Cancel]

Figure 9.13 – Creating a new function

7. Click **Create**.

8. After the creation completes, in the left menu, under **Developer**, select **Integration**. Under **Outputs**, select **+ Add output**:

Figure 9.14 – Adding output

9. Add the following values:

*   **Binding Type**: **Azure Table Storage**.

*   **Storage account connection**: Click **New** and then select the storage account that we created in the previous step.

*   **Table parameter name**: outputTable.

*   **Table name**: B2CMarketing.

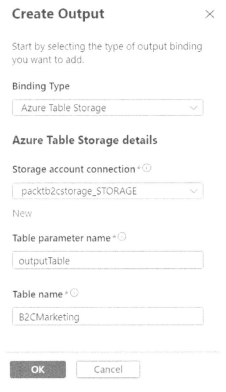

Figure 9.15 – Creating output

10. Click **OK**.

11. In the left menu, under **Developer**, select **Code + Test** and add the following code to the function app:

```
#r "Newtonsoft.Json"

using System;
using System.Net;
using System.Web;
using System.Net.Http.Formatting;
using Microsoft.AspNetCore.Mvc;
using Microsoft.Extensions.Primitives;
using Newtonsoft.Json;

public static async Task<IActionResult> Run(HttpRequest
req, ILogger log, IAsyncCollector<User> outputTable)
```

```
{
    log.LogInformation("Azure AD B2C HTTP trigger
function processed a request.");

    string requestBody = await new StreamReader(req.
Body).ReadToEndAsync();

    log.LogInformation(requestBody);

    var user = JsonConvert.
DeserializeObject<User>(requestBody);

    if (user.UserMarketing) {
        log.LogInformation("UserMarketing is true.");

        user.PartitionKey = "Users";
        user.RowKey= user.Email;

        await outputTable.AddAsync(user);
        log.LogInformation("User created.");

        return (ActionResult)new OkObjectResult($"The
user is stored." );
    }
    else {
        return (ActionResult)new OkObjectResult($"This
user doesn't want to store any info for marketing
purposes." );
    }
}
```

12. Below the `Task` method, add the following `User` class:

```
public class User {
    public string PartitionKey {get;set;}
    public string RowKey {get;set;}
    public string givenName {get;set;}
    public string surName {get;set;}
```

```
        public string Email {get;set;}
        public bool UserMarketing {get;set;}
    }
```

13. Click **Save** in the top menu.

    This code will retrieve the user information from the request, check whether the `UserMarketing` Boolean is `true`, and if so, store it in the table that we connected as the output of the function.

    Now, we need to copy the function URL to Notepad. We are going to call this URL from our custom policy that we will create in the next step.

14. In the top menu, select **Get Function URL**, and then copy the URL and paste it into a text file. This URL will also have the SAS token to connect and authenticate to the Azure function.

Now that we have both the table storage and the Azure function in place, we can start creating the custom policy.

Creating the custom policy

To create the custom policy, I've downloaded the starter package and used the `LocalAccounts` example as the base. You can download the custom policy from the GitHub folder. The download link can be obtained from the *Technical requirements* section at the beginning of this chapter.

> **Important Note**
> In this example, I've deliberately added the custom fields and Azure Functions claims provider to the `TrustFrameWorkBase.xml` file. According to the best practices, these changes need to be added to the `TrustFrameworkExtensions.xml` file to override `TrustFrameWorkBase.xml`. This makes troubleshooting and maintenance a lot easier because the base file is huge. However, to better understand where these elements need to be added to the custom policy, I've added them to the base file. I would highly recommend, for production policies, adding these changes to the `TrustFrameworkExtensions.xml` file.

Take the following steps to make the necessary changes to the custom policy files:

1. Open `TrustFrameWorkBase.xml` and change `TenantID` and `PublicPolicyUri` accordingly:

    ```
    <TrustFrameworkPolicy
      xmlns:xsi="http://www.w3.org/2001/XMLSchema-instance"
     xmlns:xsd="http://www.w3.org/2001/XMLSchema"
      xmlns="http://schemas.microsoft.com/online/cpim/
    schemas/2013/06"
      PolicySchemaVersion="0.3.0.0"
      TenantId="<yourtenant>.onmicrosoft.com"
      PolicyId="B2C_1A_TrustFrameworkBase"
      PublicPolicyUri="http://<yourtenant>.onmicrosoft.com/
    B2C_1A_TrustFrameworkBase">
    ```

2. Scroll down to line `291`. Here, you see the following lines of code, which add a checkbox to the sign-up experience:

    ```
            <ClaimType Id="UserMarketing">
                <DisplayName>UserMarketing</DisplayName>
                <DataType>boolean</DataType>
                <UserHelpText>Specifies whether the user wants to
    be added to the marketing database.</UserHelpText>
                <UserInputType>CheckboxMultiSelect</
    UserInputType>
                <Restriction>
                    <Enumeration Text="Add me to the marketing
    database to receive information." Value="true"
    SelectByDefault="true" />
                </Restriction>
            </ClaimType>
    ```

3. Next, scroll down to line 638. Here, you will see the following lines of code, which are used to call the Azure function:

```xml
<ClaimsProvider>
    <DisplayName>Function REST API</DisplayName>
     <TechnicalProfiles>
        <TechnicalProfile Id="Azurefunctions-
AddUserToTableStorage">
            <DisplayName>Add userinfo to marketing table
storage</DisplayName>
            <Protocol Name="Proprietary" Handler="Web.
TPEngine.Providers.RestfulProvider, Web.TPEngine,
Version=1.0.0.0, Culture=neutral, PublicKeyToken=null" />
            <Metadata>
                <Item Key="ServiceUrl">https://<your-function-
url>/api/AddUserToTableStorage?code=HIvCFNCgXGle17
BnrI5B0gyiDoRBM2T/JYB......Q==</Item>
                <Item Key="SendClaimsIn">Body</Item>
                <Item Key="AuthenticationType">None</Item>
            </Metadata>
            <InputClaims>
                <InputClaim
ClaimTypeReferenceId="UserMarketing"
PartnerClaimType="UserMarketing" />
                <InputClaim ClaimTypeReferenceId="givenName"
PartnerClaimType="givenName" />
                <InputClaim ClaimTypeReferenceId="surname"
PartnerClaimType="surname" />
                <InputClaim ClaimTypeReferenceId="email"
PartnerClaimType="email" />
            </InputClaims>
            <UseTechnicalProfileForSessionManagement
ReferenceId="SM-Noop" />
        </TechnicalProfile>
        </TechnicalProfiles>
    </ClaimsProvider>
```

4. Replace `ServiceUrl` with your function URL.

5. Now, save the file and open `TrustFrameworkExtensions.xml`. Again, replace `<your-domain>` inside the `BasePolicy` element accordingly:

```
<TrustFrameworkPolicy
xmlns:xsi="http://www.w3.org/2001/XMLSchema-instance"
xmlns:xsd="http://www.w3.org/2001/XMLSchema"
 xmlns="http://schemas.microsoft.com/online/cpim/
schemas/2013/06"
PolicySchemaVersion="0.3.0.0"
TenantId="<yourtenant>.onmicrosoft.com"
PolicyId="B2C_1A_TrustFrameworkExtensions"
 PublicPolicyUri="http://<yourtenant>.onmicrosoft.com/
B2C_1A_TrustFrameworkExtensions">

<BasePolicy>
  <TenantId><yourtenant>.onmicrosoft.com</TenantId>
  <PolicyId>B2C_1A_TrustFrameworkBase</PolicyId>
</BasePolicy>
```

6. Now, you can close this file and open `SignUpOrSignin.xml`. Here, you also need to replace `<yourtenant>` with the actual tenant's name in three places:

```
<TrustFrameworkPolicy
  xmlns:xsi="http://www.w3.org/2001/XMLSchema-instance"
  xmlns:xsd="http://www.w3.org/2001/XMLSchema"
  xmlns="http://schemas.microsoft.com/online/cpim/
schemas/2013/06"
  PolicySchemaVersion="0.3.0.0"
  TenantId="<yourtenant>.onmicrosoft.com"
  PolicyId="B2C_1A_signup_signin_function"
  PublicPolicyUri="http://<yourtenant>.onmicrosoft.com/
B2C_1A_signup_signin">

  <BasePolicy>
    <TenantId><yourtenant>.onmicrosoft.com</TenantId>
    <PolicyId>B2C_1A_TrustFrameworkExtensions</PolicyId>
  </BasePolicy>
```

7. We need to add the `UserMarketing` value to the claims. On line 28 you see the `UserMarketing` claim being added:

```
<RelyingParty>
    <DefaultUserJourney ReferenceId="SignUpOrSignIn" />
    <TechnicalProfile Id="PolicyProfile">
        <DisplayName>PolicyProfile</DisplayName>
        <Protocol Name="OpenIdConnect" />
        <OutputClaims>
          <OutputClaim ClaimTypeReferenceId="displayName"
/>
          <OutputClaim ClaimTypeReferenceId="givenName" />
          <OutputClaim ClaimTypeReferenceId="surname" />
          <OutputClaim ClaimTypeReferenceId="email" />
          <OutputClaim ClaimTypeReferenceId="objectId"
PartnerClaimType="sub"/>
          <OutputClaim ClaimTypeReferenceId="tenantId"
AlwaysUseDefaultValue="true"
DefaultValue="{Policy:TenantObjectId}" />
          <OutputClaim ClaimTypeReferenceId="UserMarketing"
DefaultValue="true" />

        </OutputClaims>
        <SubjectNamingInfo ClaimType="sub" />
    </TechnicalProfile>
    </RelyingParty>
```

8. Now, save the XML files.

Now that we have added the marketing checkbox and called the Azure function during the sign-up experience, we are ready to deploy the custom policy to Azure AD B2C.

Deploying the custom policy

In the last step of this demonstration, we are going to deploy the custom policy to Azure AD B2C. Because of the hierarchy of the XML files, we need to upload them in a particular order. Starting with `TrustFrameworkBase.xml`, followed by `TrustFrameworkExtensions.xml`, and lastly, the *Relying Party* file: `SignUpOrSignin.xml`:

1. In the Identity Experience Framework settings, in the left menu, select **Custom policies**.

2. Then, in the top menu, click **Upload custom policy**:

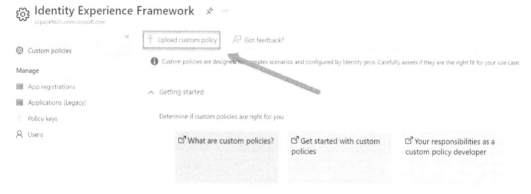

Figure 9.16 – Uploading custom policy

3. Then, upload the files in the following order:

    I.   `TrustFrameworkBase.xml`

    II.   `TrustFrameworkExtensions.xml`

    III. `SignUpOrSignin.xml`

    If you forgot to replace the tenant's name somewhere in these files, you will receive an error here. Ensure that all tenant names are replaced with your Azure AD B2C tenant name before uploading the file.

After uploading the files, we can now test them.

Testing the custom policy

We have now arrived at the final step of this demonstration. We are going to test the custom policy. For this, take the following steps:

1. On the **Custom policies** overview page, select **B2C_1A_SIGNUP_SIGNIN_ FUNCTION**. This will open the settings. Here, make sure that **PacktB2CApp**, which we registered in *Chapter 7, Introducing Azure Active Directory B2C*, is selected, and make sure that the reply URL is set to https://jwt.ms:

Figure 9.17 – Testing the custom policy

2. Select **Run now**.

3. We will now be redirected to the default sign-in page of Azure AD B2C.

4. Click **Sign up now**.

5. You will now see that the custom policy is enabled, there is a **UserMarketing** checkbox added to the sign-up page, and that it is selected by default.

6. Register a new user here. Ensure that the **UserMarketing** checkbox is checked:

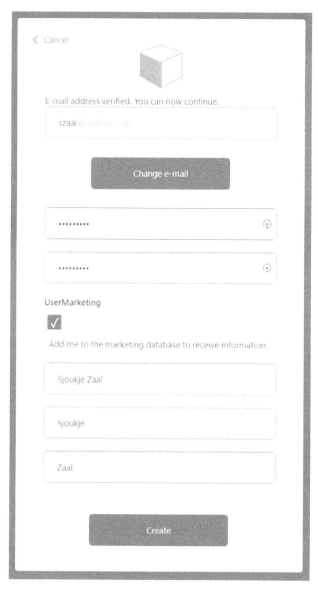

Figure 9.18 – Registering a new user

7. Click **Create**. The user account is now created inside the Azure AD B2C tenant as a local account. The custom policy will verify whether the **UserMarketing** checkbox is checked and will then make a request to the Azure function, which is going to store the user details inside the storage account. You will be redirected to `https://jwt.ms/`, where all the details will be displayed. You will notice here that the `UserMarketing` claim is added and set to `true`.

8. Navigate to the Azure storage account in the Azure portal. Don't forget to switch to the Azure AD tenant first.

9. On the **Storage account overview** page, in the left menu, select **Storage Browser (preview)**. Select **Tables**, and then select the **B2CMarketing** table.

10. There will be a row added to the table with the user profile information:

Figure 9.19 – User information added to table storage

We have now successfully added the user information to the table storage, using a custom policy in Azure AD B2C, an Azure function, and Azure Table storage. This concludes this demonstration and also this chapter.

Summary

In the last chapter of this book, we have completely focused on custom policies in Azure AD B2C. We touched on the basics, covered the Identity Experience Framework, and created our own custom policy, uploaded it to Azure AD B2C, and tested it in the Azure portal.

This concludes this book. I really hope that you enjoyed reading this book as much as I enjoyed writing it. I also hope that by reading this book, you have learned how to create and build secure applications using Azure AD and AD B2C.

Further reading

You can check out the following links for more information about the topics that were covered in this chapter:

- *Developer notes for Azure Active Directory B2C*: `https://docs.microsoft.com/en-us/azure/active-directory-b2c/custom-policy-developer-notes`

- *TrustFrameworkPolicy*: `https://docs.microsoft.com/en-us/azure/active-directory-b2c/trustframeworkpolicy`

- *Azure Active Directory B2C: Custom CIAM User Journeys*: `https://github.com/azure-ad-b2c/samples`

- *Error codes: Azure Active Directory B2C*: `https://docs.microsoft.com/en-us/azure/active-directory-b2c/error-codes`

Index

Packt.com

Subscribe to our online digital library for full access to over 7,000 books and videos, as well as industry leading tools to help you plan your personal development and advance your career. For more information, please visit our website.

Why subscribe?

- Spend less time learning and more time coding with practical eBooks and Videos from over 4,000 industry professionals

- Improve your learning with Skill Plans built especially for you

- Get a free eBook or video every month

- Fully searchable for easy access to vital information

- Copy and paste, print, and bookmark content

Did you know that Packt offers eBook versions of every book published, with PDF and ePub files available? You can upgrade to the eBook version at packt.com and as a print book customer, you are entitled to a discount on the eBook copy. Get in touch with us at customercare@packtpub.com for more details.

At www.packt.com, you can also read a collection of free technical articles, sign up for a range of free newsletters, and receive exclusive discounts and offers on Packt books and eBooks.

Other Books You May Enjoy

If you enjoyed this book, you may be interested in these other books by Packt:

Infrastructure as Code with Azure Bicep

Yaser Adel Mehraban

ISBN: 9781801813747

- Get started with Azure Bicep and install the necessary tools
- Understand the details of how to define resources with Bicep
- Use modules to create templates for different teams in your company
- Optimize templates using expressions, conditions, and loops
- Make customizable templates using parameters, variables, and functions
- Deploy templates locally or from Azure DevOps or GitHub
- Stay on top of your IaC with best practices and industry standards

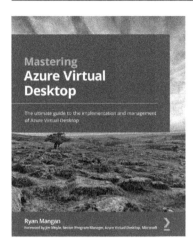

Mastering Azure Virtual Desktop

Ryan Mangan

ISBN: 9781801075022

- Design Azure Virtual Desktop and user identities and profiles
- Implement networking and storage for Azure Virtual Desktop
- Create and configure session host images and host pools
- Manage access and security for MS Azure Virtual Desktop
- Implement FSLogix Profile Containers and FSLogix Cloud Cache
- Configure user experience and Azure Virtual Desktop features
- Plan and implement business continuity and disaster recovery
- Automate Azure Virtual Desktop tasks

Packt is searching for authors like you

If you're interested in becoming an author for Packt, please visit `authors.packtpub.com` and apply today. We have worked with thousands of developers and tech professionals, just like you, to help them share their insight with the global tech community. You can make a general application, apply for a specific hot topic that we are recruiting an author for, or submit your own idea.

Share Your Thoughts

Now you've finished *Azure Active Directory for Secure Application Development*, we'd love to hear your thoughts! Scan the QR code below to go straight to the Amazon review page for this book and share your feedback or leave a review on the site that you purchased it from.

`https://packt.link/r/1838646507`

Your review is important to us and the tech community and will help us make sure we're delivering excellent quality content.

Lightning Source UK Ltd.
Milton Keynes UK
UKHW031908291222
414591UK00007B/77